Supporting mental wellbeing,
building emotional sustainability

THE SUBTLE INJURY OF INFLUENCE

Managing experiences, people and the media that affect your mental health

Amberley Meredith M.Sc.

Registered Psychologist with over 25 years experience in mental health

© Amberley Meredith 2025

Print copy: ISBN: 978-1-7640628-0-0
E-book: ISBN: 978-1-7640628-1-7

All rights reserved.

No part of this publication may be reproduced, stored in a retrieval system, or transmitted in any form or by any means—electronic, mechanical, photocopying, recording, or otherwise—without the prior written permission of the copyright owner, except for brief quotations used for the purposes of review, commentary, or scholarly work, with appropriate acknowledgement.

This publication is not a substitute for professional mental health advice or treatment. Readers experiencing distress are encouraged to seek support from a qualified mental health professional.

Published in Australia.

Protected under the Copyright Act 1968 (Cth) and applicable international laws.

For permissions or inquiries, visit:
www.adaptablesustainablepsychology.com
Editors: Kerry Laidler and Timothy Baril
Front Cover Design: Britt Wilson

Also Available in the Adaptable Sustainable Psychology Collection:

Book 1: The Subtle Injury of Influence

Managing experiences, people and media that affect your mental health

Book 2: I'm Getting There

Overcoming emotional obstacles and hidden patterns that can block change

Book 3: Self-Improvement Burnout

When to start, when to stop

Book 4: Steps Towards Kindness and Accountability

The dance of healthier relationships

Dedication:

This series is dedicated to everyone who has survived: survived pain, survived trauma, survived disappointment.

Your stories are the true history of human culture, and an integral part of our evolution.

About the Author:

Amberley Meredith has worked in the field of mental health and wellbeing for over 25 years. Her professional journey began in 1995 as a volunteer in a UK-based drug and alcohol drop-in centre. She went on to complete a Bachelor of Science in Psychology and a Master of Science in Health Psychology in the United Kingdom.

Amberley has been registered as a psychologist in both Australia and New Zealand for over 20 years. Across her career, she has worked in diverse settings including acute mental health care and working as an authorised officer, held roles in community mental health services and on a children's acquired brain injury team, run a regional eating disorder liaison service, and worked with numerous multidisciplinary teams. She has continued to operate her own clinic in private practice across most of her career, specialising more in trauma and disability for the past decade. She has designed and facilitated trauma-informed retreats and created psycho-educational programs for community and corporate environments.

Drawing on over 60,000 hours of professional practice with individuals, couples, and groups, Amberley created this self-development series to share practical strategies derived from evidence-based psychological approaches. Her work integrates knowledge from a range of therapeutic frameworks and psychology principles.

Amberley is committed to making psychological knowledge accessible and meaningful. Her educational resources are designed to support reflection, insight, and the development of emotional wellbeing in an inclusive, relatable way. Amberley is continually inspired by what people can achieve when vulnerability is met with self-belief.

Adaptable Sustainable Psychology
Disclaimer:

This content is intended for general educational and informational purposes only. It is not a substitute for professional psychological advice, diagnosis, or treatment. If you are experiencing distress or mental health concerns, please consult a registered psychologist or qualified healthcare provider.

The concepts and tools described in this series are based on psychological theory and practice but are not intended to represent or replace personalised therapeutic support. Outcomes may vary based on individual circumstances.

The exercises and questions provided are for educational and self-reflective purposes only. If at any point you feel distressed, overwhelmed, or emotionally unsettled while completing these exercises or responding to the questions, please seek support from a qualified mental health professional. This material is not a substitute for therapy or clinical intervention.

Amberley Meredith is a registered psychologist with the Australian Health Practitioner Regulation Agency (AHPRA). Her registration prohibits offering testimonials or making claims of guaranteed outcomes.

Contents

Welcome and namaste – the divine in me honours the divine in you. 1
1. Introducing Adaptable Sustainable Psychology (ASP) 17
   Exercise: Self-Calming and Grounding 24
   Pause—Reflect—Landscape 28
2. Who Am I? I Forget 33
   Exercise: "Dear Me ...". 39
   Pause—Reflect—Landscape 41
3. You Do You. 45
   Exercise: Self - Heredity - Cultural Identity............ 55
   Pause—Reflect—Landscape 58
4. Getting to You: A Map for the Voyage 63
   Exercise: Strengths Supporting Vulnerabilities........... 72
   Pause—Reflect—Landscape 74
5. Consciousness: Ego vs Awareness 79
   Exercise: Creating a Compassionate Breathwork 86
   Pause—Reflect—Landscape 89
6. Assumption is a Poor Currency 95
   Exercise: Just Being - Breathing Meditation............ 103
   Pause—Reflect—Landscape 106
7. The Illusion of Self-Phobia: A Close and Personal Danger .. 111
   Exercise: Know Your Expectations.................. 120
   Pause—Reflect—Landscape 123

8. Being an Emotional Alchemist 129
    Exercise: Musical Meditation 139
    Pause—Reflect—Landscape 141
9. In The Pursuit of Finding Balance 147
    Exercise: Balance Check-Up 153
    Pause—Reflect—Landscape 155
10. Review of Insights into You 159
    Exercise: Insights Gained into You 164
    Next Steps 166
Acknowledgments - With Gratitude 168

Welcome and namaste – the divine in me honours the divine in you.

What, you may ask, is an Adaptable Sustainable Psychology—and why would you need one?

Developing your own Adaptable Sustainable Psychology is about exploring yourself and discovering what helps keep you mentally and emotionally healthy, both now and into the future. In modern society, we can be saturated with information and at times feel the burden of the past or anxious about the future. We can feel like there is a constant demand to have an emotional response and yet, there is no space and time to do so. Adapting our psychological and emotional frameworks to evolve with these demands can help us manage them in sustainable ways. This series is designed to support self-reflection and explore how to care for your wellbeing and your relationships with others.

We all work within an emotional bandwidth which, like a muscle, can become strained if pushed too far. By understanding ourselves more intimately, we're better able to assess that bandwidth and adapt to circumstances in ways that preserve our emotional health. Protecting this emotional bandwidth may be aided by hitting the pause button, seeing the bigger picture, knowing that emotions, however intense, will pass and making relevant course corrections—even when it's hard.

What limits our ability to pause, see that bigger picture and cope with the uncomfortable moments, is where developing our Adaptable Sustainable Psychology may help.

Adaptable Sustainable Psychology draws on scientific and therapeutic principles and includes interactive exercises that encourage reflection and emotional insight. These resources invite you to explore your experiences, consider areas for growth, and develop strategies that align with your own wellbeing goals, build strength and flexibility into your emotional bandwidth.

Resilience is a concept many of us are familiar with, it is an internal skill developed over time, it is your emotional muscle. It grows from surviving difficult events and is found in the willingness to face new challenges. Most people don't realise how resilient they are until life tests them or someone else points it out. Resilience is not about emotional suppression, avoidance, or denial. It comes from moving through your emotions—not around them—and learning something in the process, becoming the psychological opportunist who can make the most of even the toughest challenges.

Developing your own Adaptable Sustainable Psychology supports the cultivation of resilience by building **psychodiversity: a s**et of personalised coping tools and tactics that help you manage emotional and psychological challenges. Think of psychodiversity as an emotional wardrobe. Just as your clothing wardrobe includes different outfits for different events, your emotional wardrobe holds a range of coping mechanisms suited to different situations. Psychodiversity helps you understand what fits you best, when to change your approach, and how to update your skills over time to stay emotionally well.

Welcome and namaste – the divine in me honours the divine in you.

Our starting point is this:
How have we become the way we are?

You probably already know that people and experiences shape how you feel. What you might not realise is how significantly systems of influence—media, advertising, politics, religion, and cultural norms—also can shape your mental and emotional health across your lifetime. Market research is a multi-billion-dollar industry, one that is continually working out how to manipulate you into buying services and products. All media systems are trying to leverage your engagement by messing with how you feel, enticing you in with drama or engaging you with shock tactics. The political systems in which we live or the religion we are part of can have a significant impact on how we see ourselves, affecting our hope for something better and our sense of self within our community.

When it comes to our mental and emotional wellbeing, we know we don't want to feel anxious or depressed. And yet, at times we do. What we may not fully understand is that these feelings may not just be reactions to our current situation. They could also stem from cumulative experiences and hidden influences that have distorted our self-image and coping strategies. There may be other influences, both positive and somewhat more insidious that may come from genetics, family dynamics, social messaging, or subtle life experiences. Much of how we see ourselves is filtered through the actions or inactions of others—often unconsciously.

One of the most powerful influences on mental health is culture. Economic, political, and religious systems all shape our sense of self and our ideas about what's possible. Political parties may sell themselves based on bringing you protection, peace and prosperity. To do that, they can tell you how every other candidate will deliver the exact opposite of these things, possibly making you feel suspicious and afraid. Advertisers may prey upon your insecurities to convince you to buy their products or services, trying to make you feel insufficient for not having something or deficient for not looking or being a certain way. The media often portrays unrealistic beauty and success standards. You can watch films or TV series where everyone looks immaculate all the time, never waking up with a hair out of place, always having perfect skin, never dropping toothpaste on their top, or gotten a thread running from their t-shirt. Social media highlights curated snapshots of others' lives, potentially leaving you feeling "less than" and alone. News outlets thrive on drama and fear, often overlooking positive progress.

Over time, these messages form a blueprint for who you think you should be—flawless, successful, always happy. This creates unrealistic internal pressures and distorts your self-worth. You may compare your real life to everyone else's highlight reel, reinforcing feelings of inadequacy. These constant comparisons can amplify anxiety and hopelessness.

There are many situations in life where you might be told how to feel, what to believe about yourself, and what to value. Yet, these external factors may not have anything to do with who you really are but could end up underpinning how you cope with everything else going on, from the small stuff to the big stuff. This accumulation of external influences may lead to internal conclusions:

- "I must be unlikeable."
- "I'm unlovable."
- "I'm a failure."

These stories are often rooted not in truth, but in distorted perceptions shaped by others or are being derived from our experiences. This book invites you to slow down and look inward. It's about interrupting those patterns and asking:

- Is this story I'm telling myself actually mine?
- Does it serve me?
- What else could be true?

When we're mentally or emotionally overwhelmed, all we want is to feel better. But quick fixes or surface-level strategies often miss the depth of what's going on. Many of our struggles stem from a complex web of past experiences and subtle influences that we've never had the chance to unpack. That's why change takes time, and why emotional healing requires a deeper, more personal approach.

The "subtle injury of influence" can accumulate slowly over time or arrive suddenly. Sometimes it's so quiet that you don't even notice it's happened. This series of books offers you a structured, guided journey to gently uncover and address those hidden influences, all within the framework of developing your own Adaptable Sustainable Psychology—a personalised, practical system for supporting your emotional wellbeing.

Important note:

This resource is not a replacement for therapy or professional mental health treatment. It is not intended to diagnose or treat mental illness. It is an educational guide to support your personal growth, increase your self-awareness, and enhance your emotional resilience.

The Adaptable Sustainable Psychology Collection

There are four books in this collection, each building on the one before. The insights gained in Book 1 carry forward into Books 2, 3, and 4. Each book includes chapters and exercises for you to complete. You may find it helpful to read one chapter at a time and then pause to spend some time reflecting on what you have read to increase your absorption of what is important or relevant to you. Go at your own pace. Skip sections if needed—but try to do the exercises in sequence to maximise benefit. You are encouraged to take your insights into therapy, coaching, or conversations with trusted friends. Talking about what you're learning will help reinforce and sustain your progress.

Book 1: The Subtle Injury of Influence

Managing experiences, people, and media that affect your mental health

This first book introduces the concept and potential value of developing your own Adaptable Sustainable Psychology in a world of rapid change and constant information flow—where the pressure to respond and keep up can feel overwhelming. It invites you to reflect on the experiences, people, and media that may have shaped how you view yourself and your wellbeing. This reflection can offer insight into how external influences affect your inner world.

You'll begin to gently map out aspects of who you are and consider how certain patterns or beliefs may have developed. This book also encourages you to explore self-compassion—what it looks like for you, and how viewing yourself through a compassionate lens can help you better understand what supports you and what doesn't.

Welcome and namaste – the divine in me honours the divine in you.

Book 2: I'm Getting There

Overcoming emotional obstacles and hidden patterns that can block change

Book 1 explores some of the influences that may have shaped your sense of self and mental wellbeing—perhaps offering insight into which habits, beliefs, or thought patterns are helpful, and which may be getting in the way. This next book focuses on gently challenging the beliefs and behaviours that may no longer serve you, using your strengths and supporting your vulnerabilities with care and compassion.

Book 2 introduces key ideas from neuroscience around how we form and change habits, particularly those that influence our emotional wellbeing. We explore ways to communicate with yourself about what you're feeling, and consider coping strategies that aim to support your wellbeing now and into the future. The goal is to begin replacing less helpful habits with more sustainable ones—building a personal emotional framework to support your growth. This phase offers a kind of scaffolding to help you cope well with life and become more self-supportive.

Book 3: Self-Improvement Burnout

When to start, when to stop

Book 3 explores the pivotal point between working to improve yourself and being okay just as you are. Feeling that you're enough can create space for accountability, better long-term decisions, and healthier boundaries. Self-acceptance may also make it easier to acknowledge mistakes without losing your sense of self-worth—and that can contribute to greater emotional resilience.

We take a look at mindfulness—a wellbeing classic for a

reason. While it isn't a one-size-fits-all tool, and there can be real blocks to practicing it, for many people it offers a helpful way to anchor themselves during challenging moments and engage more fully with pleasant ones. This phase is about reconstruction and integration—building on the foundations of self-acceptance and weaving those insights into everyday life in ways that feel practical and supportive.

Book 4: Steps Towards Kindness and Accountability

The dance of healthier relationships

To build meaningful relationships with others, it can help to reflect on your own needs while also recognising the needs of those around you. Developing a clear sense of self may support you in managing stress and self-doubt—allowing you to feel more grounded and comfortable being yourself. With this emotional steadiness, you may find it easier to navigate interactions more thoughtfully and consider the bigger picture of what's happening between you and others.

Exploring what a balanced relationship means to you, and noticing how expectations can sometimes affect collaboration or cohesion, can help relationships feel more in sync—more like dancing together than stepping on each other's toes. By becoming more mindful of power dynamics and using communication to carefully balance responsibility, you may begin to create more mutually supportive connections. This represents a shift from a purely individual focus of "I deserve, I am entitled" toward the broader collective intention of "what supports both me and those around me." This is the social construction and integration phase, where your self-awareness becomes part of how you connect with others.

Welcome and namaste – the divine in me honours the divine in you.

The Voyage into You – Instructions for the Journey

We provide these guidelines in each of our books to help support you and remind you of how to get the most out of the material. This work is in no way meant to replace active therapy, nor is it prescribed to fix serious psychological problems that require the support and help of a trained professional.

There are many ways that you might use this work. You may be using it on your own or as a couple. You could be a professional therapist using it with a client. You might even choose to do it with a small group of friends, or make it part of your professional organisation's wellbeing program. Whichever way you pick, take your time with it. It's designed to help you run the marathon, not win the sprint. The skills taught here take a long time to develop. By that, we do mean years. If you are seeking the quick fix then, sadly, this is not going to meet that desire. The human brain may take a very long time to integrate new ways of being into an automatic habit, it requires extensive repetition and focus, but the pay offs from staying the course could be well worth the effort. **Patience, repetition and commitment need to be your companions**.

If you're someone who has been exposed to trauma, please be gentle and patient with yourself throughout the recovery journey. You may require professional support and help from qualified therapists to fully understand all the psychological, emotional, neurological and physiological impacts of trauma. Whilst the techniques discussed throughout this collection of books have relevance to anyone who has suffered trauma, due to the potentially serious impacts on the structures of the brain, mind and body, you are advised to seek additional professional help.

It is always wise to approach any therapeutic care you undertake with an attitude of being kind and gentle with yourself, knowing that extensive damage may require an extensive healing period, and just because one technique doesn't suit you, it doesn't mean there is not another pathway that might work better for you. Perhaps consider approaching your healing with a commitment to finding a way to support yourself and learning to adapt with whatever has happened, mitigating and managing the impacts, whilst finding a way to open yourself up to the joys and pleasures in life that could also be available. The powerful impact of trauma or pain may be inescapable, but the strength of your capacity to overcome it can be altered.

Take a check-in each time you pick up this book, pausing to ask yourself where your level of coping is at today. Remember, there may be areas that could be triggering and difficult. If you're feeling too busy, exhausted, or even a bit too overwhelmed, you may need to come back to it at another time. Keep doing this throughout each section, making sure you are in a receptive space to sit with what is being opened up for you. You might want to set yourself up with some quiet time. You will need pens or pencils to write with. You can write all over the book if you so wish; have fun writing in the margins! Repetition may support you in how you learn and integrate ideas and new behaviours. Reading this book once probably isn't going to lead to absorbing all the information or ideas you may find useful. Read it, reread it again, and then maybe re-read again sometime later. Keep coming back to conversations about what you have read and the insights you may experience, both in your own mind and when talking with others. This may help support and reinforce your learning.

Welcome and namaste – the divine in me honours the divine in you.

Self-development can be an interactive and two-way journey. Where it involves the intersections of other people's actions, thoughts, and feelings with our own. Whether they be positive or negative, and no matter where that interaction comes from, be it a person, the media, from a therapist, or even from a book, change may come from the place where we meet with someone else's ideas or views, and we consciously choose what might help us on our way to feeling better.

The exercises and questions given in these books are for educational and self-reflective purposes only. If at any point you feel distressed, overwhelmed, or emotionally unsettled while completing any of these exercises or reflecting on the questions asked, please seek support from a qualified mental health professional. This material is not a substitute for therapy or clinical intervention. The exercises are derived from a vast number of evidence-based therapies and wellbeing theories, including neuroscience, mindfulness, polyvagal theory, hope psychology, positive psychology, acceptance and commitment therapy, cognitive behavioural therapy, solution and emotion focused therapies, and psychology from a trauma-informed perspective.

The tools are likely to work differently for different kinds of people in different situations. Sometimes, a slight shift in the format works better for one person than another. There is no one kind of psychological or healing modality that fixes everything for everyone. But by working with a wide range of ideas, methods, and people, you may find the parts that resonate with you and adapt what does not. This is how you can build your psychodiversity for coping through life's challenges.

Many of the approaches discussed in this collection of books may have a more neurotypical focus but could be possibly modified to suit those coming from neurodivergent space. Remember, the information and techniques given are not about a prescription, but guidance to help you on your journey of finding what works for you and what supports you in feeling comfortable to be you. Play with the suggestions given, alter the exercises to work for you, however your brain interacts with the world, be it through a neurodivergent lens or a neurotypical one.

Alexithymia is a neuropsychological phenomenon, also known as emotional blindness, it is a personality trait that makes it difficult to experience, identify, understand, and express emotions. The term comes from Greek roots meaning "no words for emotions". Those who have alexithymia may find that they experience emotions through physical sensations, behaviours (including risk taking ones), as a somatic/bodily response (such as pain, tension, tingling) or in other unique ways, and they may find it helpful to learn to acknowledge these experiences in lieu of feeling their emotions.

If you have alexithymia, you can still work out what your signals and signs are that indicate you are having an emotional reaction or response, and you may be able to develop ways to respond to the experience. It may work for you to ameliorate emotional experiences with responses or cues such as massage, drumming, tapping, exercise, eating appropriately, or talking about the situation with a solution focused perspective. For example, if anger and hurt are expressed in risk taking behaviour such as driving too fast or wanting to hurt yourself, you could take up boxing and have a punching bag at home and when the urge to speed or hurt yourself arises divert yourself to the somewhat safer choice of using the punching bag. You could use an exercise bike to ride as fast as possible; you could run or walk as fast as possible or use a virtual reality game that requires you to fight. Anything that you feel may help you work through the emotion and safely process it.

Please also note, that as we use some guided imagery work in these books those with aphantasia, a cognitive phenomenon that describes the difficulty or inability to voluntarily create visual mental images, may need to look at pictures to help evoke the same connections or feelings.

Before you begin this journey, we invite you to please take a moment of stillness and a singular, deep breath. Bring yourself fully into this moment. Whenever you pick up this book, repeat this process so that you can check that you are ready to engage fully with what you are reading and get the most out of the material. Please remember, this book is not meant as a replacement for professional therapy. You can use it alongside a program of professional treatment or as part of your own personal growth.

1. Introducing

Adaptable
Sustainable
Psychology

In this section you will be learning about:

- → Why, when it comes to healing, it helps to know what has gotten you to this point.
- → How the concepts of adaptability and sustainability may help us with our emotions and psychology.
- → Why feeling we are not good enough is unsustainable.

You will need:

- ✓ A readiness to explore yourself and how you have been operating in life.
- ✓ Pen and paper to make notes on any insights that arise (you can also write in the margins!)
- ✓ To be open to discussing your reactions, feelings, and ideas, either with yourself or others.

1. Introducing Adaptable Sustainable Psychology (ASP)

When the internal battle to feel that you are enough is won,
you can own who you are.
You can grow who you are.
Then there may be peace from within.
The drive to take is replaced by the capacity to give.
In this space we adapt, we sustain. We are being well.
Not just as an individual, but together as a collective.
          Adaptable Sustainable Psychology

The world may fill us with opinions, ideas, and attitudes about ourselves. But do we stop often enough to ask what we would like to feel, be, or experience? Do we take enough time to choose how we wish to see and support ourselves? The programming that comes with being human, whether that shows up through genetics, neural pathways, social conditioning or marketing can leave us heavily influenced, potentially with an attitude that is inviting us to seek superiority, not finding self-acceptance or practicing humility. This can leave little room for a much-needed conscious and co-operative way of being. As a race, for us to move from surviving alone to thriving together, perhaps we need to start by learning how to feel good enough to simply be ourselves. Then from a deeper place of self-acceptance, we can embrace a clear commitment to finding growth from all our experiences and work harmoniously alongside one another.

But how do we feel good enough after trauma, after we are told by others that we are not worth it? When adverts are telling us we need a new product or service to be happy, safe, successful, or likeable? How do we sustain ourselves to keep this feeling of being enough throughout our lives when there is always something new to cope with? Could learning how to adapt responsively and find sustainable ways of coping that suit us help strengthen our ability to care for ourselves and others and enhance our capacity for wellbeing?

Before we commence exploring ourselves and start the discovery of what is working for us and what is not, we may benefit from knowing what healthier management of our feelings looks like. For example, it is all well and good to say that drinking won't fix your problems but perhaps having some ideas on what might help you feel better could make giving up drinking a whole lot easier. Throughout this work, we will oscillate between understanding what is not helping us and feeling out what might. Constructing a building without any scaffolding in place to support it will likely lead to the building collapsing. So, whilst investigating any subtle injuries we may have received through the various influences we have been exposed to, we will also look at some positive coping structures so we can work towards maintaining our own sense of wellbeing.

Adaptability and Sustainability:

In 1987, the United Nations Brundtland Commission defined sustainability as "meeting the needs of the present without compromising the ability of future generations to meet their own

1. Introducing Adaptable Sustainable Psychology (ASP)

needs." Sustainability, in terms of our environment and our way of living, has become our zeitgeist. Sustainability operates on the idea that resources are finite and, therefore, we need to be aware of how they are managed. Sustainability essentially creates a feedback loop where we are always putting back into the system rather than just continually taking from it. It recognises that anything unsustainable affects the whole system and is not desirable. Interestingly, we are yet to extend and apply this concept of sustainability to our internal world and the attitude with which we approach ourselves, others, and life. Surely, developing a system that can meet our present need, but which also protects us and others from future harm, would be a highly logical and sensible approach to adopt? In the modern world we can often feel that we are not enough or that we do not have enough, which can lead us into positively striving to better ourselves and our situation. But it can also become unmanaged or mismanaged and lead us into unsustainable practices that can affect both our current wellbeing, and our future wellbeing and that of others.

When we do not feel enough, we often seek more: more money, more resources, more fame, more youth, etc. The individual who moves from enhancing their looks to trying to hide them with cosmetic products and procedures can end up believing that they can't leave the house without them, all in a bid to become an influenced idea of being beautiful. But they can only do this until they run out of money, or the treatments start to adversely affect their health or works against their self-esteem, making them feel less without them. It simply is not sustainable. We can all think of a celebrity, indeed perhaps one we've admired for their creativity, skill, or talent, who has dramatically changed their appearance to fit some kind of perfected ideal. There is absolutely nothing wrong at all in wanting to change our appearance or make the best of our features. But when our self-worth is reliant on achieving some unrealistic ideal that could damage our body, our finances, or how we feel about ourselves, then vanity is overriding sanity.

There are many other examples of us practicing unsustainable habits that can ultimately harm us, some are obvious and some are more subtle. A drug user keeps injecting more heroin to get a better hit until their veins collapse, or they run out of money or friends to help them. A business owner keeps expanding their company and exhausting their staff while over capitalising on luxury cars and new tech, only to end up bankrupt or simply burnt out from the stress of managing it all. A trauma survivor drinks alcohol to numb their pain until their liver gives up, until they consume enough alcohol that they become depressed and feel suicidal, or so angry that they disregard the safety and wellbeing of themselves and others. Those who work excessive hours or are always exercising, using adrenaline to feel alive and undistracted by their past or their pain, but neglect their other relationships can end up alone and burned out both physically and mentally. There are many ways in which we are using unsustainable practices to cope with trauma or living modern life, practices that could damage us, other people, and the planet.

To support us in protecting our wellbeing, it may help to become skilled at adapting and changing unsustainable practices. By doing so, we can build a foundation for coping that fits our individual circumstances. This creates our own adaptable, sustainable psychology—one that can guide us in coping with whatever has happened, whatever comes our way, and in flexing and changing as needed to care for our future selves.

1. Introducing Adaptable Sustainable Psychology (ASP)

Psychodiversity:

The concept of psychodiversity was discussed by Apter in 1989, where he suggested that humans switch between motivational states to realise their potential and excel. This basically means we change to get the best possible outcome. Biodiversity refers to the variety of plant and animal life in the world or a particular habitat. A high level of biodiversity is important and desirable because each part contributes to support other parts, benefiting the whole system. Psychodiversity is the variety of ways we have of seeing, being, and coping to manage whatever we experience that affects our wellbeing (Semeiotike 2009). From having numerous ways of managing situations, we may support ourselves, potentially protect our finite coping resources and be more able to contribute to those around us. Having a high level of psychodiversity would look like someone who is aware of what is not serving them and then adapts in accordance with this, who is able to be present and thus manage their emotions without becoming overwhelmed, acting without creating a cost to their future self. This type of a broad, flexible foundation for coping would provide us with different approaches to challenges and enable us to move the goalposts (adapting) as needed to ensure our resources are protected (sustainability).

This inbuilt **psychological flexibility** found in the psychodiverse mind may help create space for you to fully explore yourself, other people, and opportunities available in each moment. In being flexible and able to adapt your mind, you might become more aware of when a new direction needs to be taken to increase the chances of a more **peaceful and productive** outcome, both in the short-term and in the long-term. Most of us will, at various points in our life, use unsustainable coping mechanisms to create avoidance or distraction from our problems. Or, we may engage in denial and diversion tactics to escape our feelings. We can all develop internal negative narratives that may cause harm to ourselves and deplete our finite energy resources thanks to the subtle injury of influence that we live with in this world.

But, when you abuse and berate yourself for mistakes, or put yourself down for how you look, act, or for what you do, you are likely to become drained. Through disparaging comments aimed at yourself, you can generate a feeling of not being good enough and may make yourself feel anxious or depressed. This ongoing negative narrative and the feelings it generates then fatigues you, perhaps to the point that you can no longer identify what is unhealthy. You may then lack the energy or cognitive capacity to exert the effort required to change this horrible habit of being self-abusive. Self-abuse is a habit worth giving up.

Creating psychodiversity for yourself:

To build your psychodiversity, you can begin by reflecting on how you currently respond to life's challenges. This can help you identify your strengths and vulnerabilities—noticing what supports you, and what might be contributing to current discomfort or have the potential to create difficulties in the future. From there, you can begin to gently evolve the patterns that may no longer serve you or that could unintentionally affect others. Through this self-knowledge, you may find that you can:

- Make more informed choices that align with your values and needs

1. Introducing Adaptable Sustainable Psychology (ASP)

- Recognise and manage personal vulnerabilities that could leave you feeling exposed
- Identify patterns of self-critical thinking and begin to respond with more balanced perspectives
- Notice when others may be influencing your emotional state and assess whether that influence is helpful
- Reflect on past influences that may have shaped your beliefs, and explore ways to minimise their impact going forward

Exercise: Self-Calming and Grounding

As we move into a space of deep self-reflection throughout the Adaptable Sustainable Psychology collection, we may explore topics that feel activating or emotionally challenging at times. It can be helpful to practice self-soothing and calming strategies that support emotional regulation. These skills may assist you in returning to a sense of balance, allowing you to engage with the reflections and explore meaningful pathways forward.

If you are currently managing mental health challenges or have experienced trauma, it may be beneficial to seek support from a qualified mental health professional while working through this material. This book is not a substitute for professional therapy, nor is it intended as a treatment for mental health conditions. It is an educational resource designed to support self-awareness, skill-building, and personal development.

The following section offers a selection of soothing, calming, and grounding strategies to explore before beginning the deeper work. You are invited to try these techniques and discover which, if any, help you feel calmer or more centred when experiencing emotional discomfort.

Self-Soothing

These behaviours are designed to support you in feeling comforted, calm, and grounded. They are practices that can help you develop a sense of conscious control and internal steadiness, particularly during times of emotional activation or distress. You may already use some of these behaviours without realising it. The aim here is to help you identify and intentionally use these soothing supports when needed, becoming more active in your self-care and recognising what you are doing to support yourself in challenging moments.

1. **Identify:** Tune into your body and notice which physical sensations, postures, or movements feel calming or grounding. This might include crossing your legs, sitting on the floor, gently swaying or rocking, tapping your arm, placing a hand on your belly, holding your forearms, playing with an object like a watch or ring, stroking your clothing or the chair you're sitting on, gently scratching your scalp, touching your face, or twirling your hair. These small actions can serve as self-soothing behaviours. If you're unsure which ones feel helpful to you, try out a few from this list or see if they inspire your own ideas.

2. **Practice:** Consciously use your preferred self-soothing actions during moments of emotional discomfort.

3. **Experiment:** Try different approaches to find what works best for you.

4. **Integrate:** Make your chosen techniques part of your daily self-care, using them often.

Vagus Nerve Stimulation

The vagus nerve connects the brain to many other parts of the body and plays a role in regulating digestion, heart rate, and aspects of the immune system. According to polyvagal theory, we may be able to influence vagal tone, and support emotional regulation, through certain calming activities. Some examples of activities that may influence vagal tone include:

- **Humming Bee Breath (Bhramari Pranayama):** A yoga breathing technique. Place your hands gently over your ears, close your eyes, and hum softly for 7 deep breaths.
- **Music and Movement:** Choose an upbeat song and move in a way that feels ok for you, wave your hands, dance gently, or shift from foot to foot. Let your body guide you.
- **Yoga with Breath Awareness:** Engaging in regular yoga practice, especially with focused breathwork, has been linked to increased heart rate variability (HRV), a marker of vagal tone. This practice may support emotional resilience and overall wellbeing. There are many styles of yoga that could suit your capacity when carrying out this reflective work, from gentle chair yoga to the more easeful restorative yoga, or the supportive style of yin yoga to the flowing dynamics of vinyasa yoga. Do some research and see if you could access one through a class or on-line resource.

1. Introducing Adaptable Sustainable Psychology (ASP)

Gentle Ear or Neck Massage:

- **Ear Massage:** With slow, deep breathing, use slow, circular motions behind your earlobes, at the base of your ears, or around the outer ear cartilage—areas thought to be linked to vagal nerve pathways.
- **Neck Massage:** With slow, deep breathing, gently massage the sides of your neck from the collarbone upwards, paying attention to anywhere you notice tension.

Super Simple Breathwork

This basic and easy-to-remember breathwork practice may offer grounding and comfort during difficult moments. While it might feel subtle at first, repeating it over several minutes may increase its effectiveness.

1. As you breathe in, count "1."
2. As you breathe out, count "2."
3. Continue this pattern at a comfortable pace until you begin to feel more grounded and calmer.

Pause — Reflect — Landscape

We are working on developing our own Adaptable Sustainable Psychology, so we may learn how to help ourselves feel better, treat ourselves better and treat others better. At the end of each section, we want to reinforce and integrate any new knowledge. Reflecting on the material in relation to ourselves and our life will help with this, and, where relevant, show us where we may adjust accordingly.

1. Pause - Take a moment to sit with what you have just learned and consider it.

- To become a more cohesive and collaborative society, we first need to feel good enough being ourselves.
- We may be subtly and adversely influenced by people, experiences and the media. Understanding if and how this has happened can help us manage self-doubt and reduce the impact of limiting beliefs.
- Being able to adapt to situations and select sustainable ways to cope could help us in the moment and enhance our capacity for future wellness.
- Having clear ideas on how to handle our emotions well aids us in changing the things that are either unhelpful or harmful for us.

- Being psychodiverse keeps us mentally flexible and gives us access to numerous ways to manage life well.
- Creating our own psychodiversity, away from any unhelpful external influences, gives us a toolbox to face problems with and equips us to be able to encourage and support ourselves through difficulties, rather than abusing ourselves with harsh judgment and self-criticism.
- Developing our own Adaptable Sustainable Psychology allows us to learn helpful coping mechanisms that suit us and maximise, not deplete, resources. Enabling us to support our mental health and emotional resilience.

2. Reflect - Answer the following questions:

- What is your reaction to the idea that you may have been adversely influenced by experiences, the media and other people into feeling negatively about yourself?
- How do you feel about the concept of developing your own adaptable sustainable psychology to help you cope with life and minimise risks to your future self and others?
- Did any of the self-calming exercises resonate with you? How do you feel about consciously using them on a daily basis?

3. Landscape – Take a step back to see how this new information fits in with the bigger picture of your life. Consider your history, what is going on for you now, who and what is in your life, and the future you want for yourself.

- ✓ Can you identify times in your life where you may have

been adversely influenced by experiences, people or the media?

- ✓ Are you someone who adapts well to changes and challenges, or can you see times when you have struggled in the past, or do you get anxious about the future?
- ✓ How do you think you have managed your emotions previously? Has this caused you issues in the past, in the present or could cause you problems in the future?

2.

Who Am I? I Forget

In this section you will be learning about:

- → What is important about our identity in terms of being able to be adaptable and sustainable.
- → Where can our identity take us? Self-focused versus self-forgetting.
- → How self-focus can lead us to feel we are not enough, and self-forgetting can empower us to be enough.

You will need:

- ✓ A willingness to take stock of the involvement you have with yourself, and of how much you consider others.
- ✓ To be open to discussing your reactions, feelings, and ideas, either with yourself or others.

2. Who Am I? I Forget

"The surest way to lose your self-worth is by trying to find it through the eyes of others."

Becca Lee

We are a tapestry of our experiences, emotions, interactions, values and beliefs. Our identity is a journey from our conception to our death. It is constantly being influenced. We shift and change with our roles, environments, and feelings. To give you an analogy, when taking a single car journey, you can leave your home with a clear idea of who you are and be feeling good, only to listen to a song that brings you into a state of sadness because it is connected to a lost relationship from years before. As you travel on, you see a building that reminds you of your childhood, and it brings another completely different feeling, perhaps excitement or wonder. Eventually, you arrive at your destination to meet up with a colleague, and you shift into your serious work persona.

Identity is fluid, and influenced by both your internal and external worlds. To help support how our identities flow, and be able to traverse the many directions they might take us in, having knowledge about each of these identities and what kind of person we are at our core can be useful. You can have many ways of being, different identities, but they are still all you. You could, for example, own many different types of cars, but their purpose is fundamentally the same, to get you from one place to another. As we move from one experience to another, accepting each facet of ourselves and being aware of how that might help or possibly harm us in any given situation may assist us in navigating life. Our identities are a key part of how we form our psychodiversity as we can tailor coping mechanisms to suit the different needs of our different identities. If we learn to use our **identity as a vehicle** that we can drive, we can consciously choose which part of us to activate in different situations. Recognising that, just as a four-wheel-drive handles terrain differently than a sports car, we can learn how our identities can handle different circumstances.

The Self-Forgetting Identity vs The Self-Focussed Identity

At times, the seemingly ongoing barrage of life that we must deal with can feel like an unrelenting parade. This is possibly why self-help has become one of the biggest markets in our world today. There is an abundance of books, techniques, healing protocols, and rituals available. This is all in the pursuit of the elusive, improved self. Unfortunately, it can often be the case that the more we look at ourselves, the more confusing it might become. A healthy, happy, and grounded individual has no need to put themselves down, or make others feel bad, nor to take advantage of people. The individual who feels they are enough, and they have enough, does not need to hurt themselves or take anything from others. They have an awareness of who they are and an awareness of those around them. They understand their impact upon themselves and others, and act accordingly.

This could all sound so simple: be healthy, grounded, and

happy. But just because something seems simple it does not make it easy. Self-development is the very epitome of the seemingly simple being deceivingly complex. One of the dangers of self-development could be unconsciously engaging with the idea that you have fixed yourself, your identity becoming one of "I've done all the work"—indicating to yourself and others there is nothing else you need do, only to find a new problem raises another aspect of yourself that you had not even realised could be an issue. The thought of reaching a final destination or utopia of perfected existence is a seductive idea. However, life does not stop throwing challenges at you, and what has worked in the past may one day no longer be relevant or might harm you or others. This means you may have to utilise different identities to help you manage how you cope, interchanging and evolving each of them as your life changes and balancing the focus between yourself and others.

A new design does not necessarily mean the final design. Take, for example, the first petrol cars, which revolutionised the way we lived and travelled, but which we now understand are harming our planet, and so they are being evolved to cause less harm. Your coping identity is the same. It is helpful to keep upgrading yourself in relation to the changing world around you and within you. An evolving psychodiversity enables you to keep adapting, and therefore sustaining yourself, throughout your life. Inevitably, that means who you are will keep changing. Just as cars are evolving not only to suit individuals but also to be more mindful of the physical environment, we too might need to evolve our identities in relation to others as well as ourselves, at times forgetting ourselves to pay attention to those around us.

Self-development is all about the well-being of you. It

is entirely focussed on the self. The Cambridge Dictionary explains the act of self-forgetting is to forget about yourself and your own interests. It states the focus is on other people's needs and wants rather than just your own. A bit too much "it's all about me" is as equally unhelpful as "always put others first". There would seem to be a delicate balance that we must seek between being **self-focused and self-forgetting**. Managing this balance may help us to manage the various life experiences we have. But in a world where self-identity is expounded through multiple mediums, including advertising and social media, where dynamics such as "I deserve" or "I am entitled to" are elevated as ideals, does this get in the way of being truly self-forgetful?

Now that we have so many apps, labour-saving devices, and methods of entertainment available, it is almost as if there is no respite or time to just be. Social media can spark a singular focus on the self with engagement being measured by a like or a dislike. Comments may be monologues, as opposed to dialogues. When something is posted and not well received, the feeling of not being good enough could be echoed and amplified. The downside of this kind of single self-focused environment is that it doesn't encourage us into self-forgetting. Everything in moderation is a well-known quote, and it still has relevance today. Self-development can become too all consuming, and we forget to develop with those alongside us, leaving us potentially feeling lonely and isolated, despite working on ourselves.

Self-forgetting may be the soothing balm needed to balance out looking after ourselves and caring for those around us. Then, in these moments when we consider others, we also can see reflections of ourselves that we either might like or dislike. We could discover aspects of our own behaviour that might push people away or not build trust, showing us perhaps why we have been experiencing unhappiness or anxiety in our relationships. In considering others, we may find deeper joys in giving rather than receiving, creating a sense of satisfaction that might have previously been unavailable to us. We might realise we are a caring and kind individual and not the terrible person we believed we are who is always to blame.

Whilst one aspect of self-forgetting is thinking about and doing things for others, it is also about being in the moment. Something as simple as appreciating nature, enjoying the colour of the sky, reading a book that makes you laugh, or listening to your friends having fun without it involving you, would be good examples of self-forgetting. It might allow you to immerse in the moment, so both you and the moment are then enough. No embellishment or acknowledgment of the self is needed. By being in control of our ability to enjoy what is around us, we could facilitate the letting go of being controlling. So, instead of trying to influence others and how they perceive us, or influencing ourselves to make the moment more perfect, we just get on with enjoying it.

You might fear that self-forgetting will lead you to ignore important lessons from your past. By putting others' needs and wants first, do I risk being taking advantage of? Will I forget how I have been hurt before, and thus expose myself to the risk of being hurt again in the same way? If you rely on pain to help you navigate, you may risk compromising yourself. When you are in pain, you are more likely to become overwhelmed and feel vulnerable. Being overwhelmed could lead you to either not being able to act or to make a choice that does not work for you. Neuroscientific research indicates that when self-forgetting is engaged, our performance and capacity is enhanced and improved, not lessened. This may suggest that if you are able to self-forget the part of you that was hurt from the experience, while also maintaining awareness of what happened, it could support you in making more informed choices that may reduce the likelihood of similar situations occurring in the future. You can keep an eye out for risks with a clear head. By knowing your identities well, and that identity is fluid, you can switch into the self-forgetful identity appropriately and look to the other person's needs and wants, and you can flick back into your self-focused identity to check that this resonates with you, is fair on you, and about co-operation and not manipulation.

The benefits of balancing between forgetting yourself and focusing on yourself seem to outweigh the hyper-focus on the idealized self. The potential payoffs are **a better internal relationship with yourself** and **a better external relationship with others**. Self-forgetting leads us towards a concept of collective development and a helpful self-development. Balancing self-forgetting with self-focus is a challenge, and it is going to take practice and time. A monk in training will retreat to a monastery for many years to learn these kinds of skills. They can spend years in caves meditating, away from the influences and effects of society, culture, conditioning, and other people's agendas. Trying to learn the skills required to adapt and sustain through life when living amongst such vast and complex populations is about as challenging as it gets. Give yourself time to learn this, and be patient with the process.

Exercise: "Dear Me ..."

As you begin the reflective practice of looking inward and starting this journey, it may help to dedicate a special file, folder, or even a specific journal for any written exercises you undertake. This way, you can keep all your insights and reflections in one place and more clearly track your progress.

Writing a letter to yourself may be a helpful tool for gaining insight into how you currently see yourself, how you look after yourself, and how you feel about who you are. This approach won't work for everyone, and that's okay, it may be something you try and find isn't quite the right fit for you. You might only write a few lines, or it could turn into a page or two. The amount you write is not important; the content is what will be meaningful as you move through the Adaptable Sustainable Psychology collection. There is no right or wrong way to do this exercise.

Be mindful of any negative self-judgment that might arise. If this exercise doesn't look or feel the way you think it "should," choose to be kind to yourself instead. Remember, we will explore other exercises throughout these books to support your understanding of yourself.

To begin:

- Sit down in a quiet, private place where you are unlikely to be disturbed.
- Turn off your phone and free yourself as much as possible from external distractions.
- Using pen and paper (which is preferable to typing on a device), begin writing a letter to yourself.

In your letter, consider expressing:

- How you currently see yourself
- How you think you look after yourself in terms of self-care
- What it feels like to be you
- What you like or dislike about being you

If you find this exercise brings up difficult emotions, please pause and consider seeking support from a therapist or mental health professional.

Pause—Reflect—Landscape

1. Pause - Take a moment to sit with what you have just learned and consider it.

- Identity is multi-faceted, fluid and changes across our lives. Our identities are influenced by our external world, others or our choices.
- We have an identity that can manage how we cope with life, and we can take control of this identity and shape it according to what will work best for us, and others, both in the now and the long-term.
- To self-forget is to forget about ourselves and our own interests and focus on other people's needs and wants. It is also about being in the moment and being present with whatever is happening without needing self-involvement.
- To self-focus is to pay attention to our own needs, manage appropriate self-care and protect ourselves with prior experience and knowledge to support outcomes that align with our values and goals.
- Being self-focused is helpful when developing and growing who we are, but we also need to be self-forgetful, moving between these two identities to grow and evolve.

- Patience is required when working with ourselves and seeking change and balance.

2. Reflect - Answer the following questions:

- Do you resonate with the idea that we have multiple identities that we move in and out of in our lives?
- Are you someone who comfortably switches from self-focus to being self-forgetful? Do you experience imbalances in either identity, where you over give to others or pay too much attention to yourself at the expense of others?
- Is being patient something that comes naturally to you or are you someone who prefers quick results?

3. Landscape - Take a step back to see how this new information fits in with the bigger picture of your life. Consider your history, what is going on for you now, who and what is in your life, and the future you want for yourself.

- ✓ Can you see times during your life where you have changed your identify to suit a situation? Did this help improve things or cause problems?
- ✓ Are there some new identities that you could evolve within yourself that might help you deal better with certain types of situations?
- ✓ If being patient is not your best skill, do you have any ideas on how you could improve this or will you need outside help to manage the slow process of change?

3.

You Do You.

In this section you will be learning about:

- → Why it is important to take time to fully know ourselves.
- → How gathering information about ourselves forms a foundation for change.
- → Why daily information overload is affecting our health and wellbeing.
- → How our mind can work from different spaces and how this affects us.

You will need:

- ✓ A pen and paper.
- ✓ The willingness to honest about all sides of yourself.
- ✓ Time and space to complete a written exercise.
- ✓ To be open to discussing your reactions, feelings, and ideas, either with yourself or others.

3. You Do You.

"If you know who you are, no one can convince you to be who you are not."

                                             Matshona Dhliwayo

"You do you" is pop-cult saying here in Australia. It is an interesting take on the self-focus versus self-forgetful dynamic. However, how does one do "you do you" when you do not fully know who you are? Whilst some people may be fond of this phrase, there are those who will take actions that set parameters about how they need or want you to be, meaning it is more about how they want you to do you. If you do not fully know yourself, or if you are insecure, then "you doing you" could become challenging. Sometimes, it is even impossible when you cannot clearly ascertain who you are amongst the noise of the influences and pressures of those around you and the roles you feel you are being asked to play. This leads to the unhelpful kind of self-forgetting, because you have forgotten who you are to the extent that you then compromise yourself and put your resources into deficit for the sake of others.

Information can be one of your best allies. Gaining self-information may be helpful when you are looking at how to change. When a country goes to war, they do not drop their troops in the middle of anywhere, and hope for the best. They gather intel—collecting information, researching vulnerabilities that could pose a threat, and finding strengths that can be used as an advantage. This is a useful strategy that you can apply to your different identities. If you gather information about who you are, and why you operate in certain ways, you discover what is helpful or unhelpful, which may be advantageous in taking care of your wellbeing. You can identify influences that both nurture you and potentially cause you harm. All of this gives you a foundation to start navigating between awareness of when you might need to self-forget and when you need to self-focus. "Doing you" in consideration of others may then feel more manageable.

Who am I again?

When you are well cared for by yourself, you may find that this leaves you feeling freer to find space to care well for others. That is the essence of sustainability. What you put into your life feeds back and creates the flow of life. This first piece of work can help you to gain information and insights into you. It can help you understand yourself at a deeper level, including how you have become this way. You may then be able to gather information to help you answer the following.

- How do I identify what works for me and what doesn't serve me?
- How do I work out better ways of caring for myself?
- How do I make space for others and care well for them?

A world with an ever-increasing population naturally only becomes more competitive. This means you can easily be distracted by the noise and clutter of everyone else's identity, their influences, their needs, and their wants. As a result, you

3. You Do You.

may end up mirroring or adopting ways of being that might not necessarily work for you. In amongst this noise of everyone else, your self-identity may fight harder and louder to be seen and heard. Then you could become so competitively self-focused that you only promote your identity as a singular dimension, for example, I am a lawyer; I am a mother; I am an athlete; etc., to others, as well as to yourself. We push to be the most unique, the most talented, the prettiest, the fittest, or the most successful. We want to have the most likes on TikTok or the most followers on Instagram. The downside of all this is then you limit yourself to one identity, and it's probably an identity that does not work for you in every circumstance. It puts your future potentially at risk if, for any reason, one day you cannot be in that role or hold that identity, who are you then? Singularity does not promote psychodiversity. This could leave you vulnerable to acting in ways that are not helpful or do not provide the growth that you need to cope with all the invariable challenges and changes in life.

In the modern world, we are quite literally flooded with information and stimulation like never before. Scientists believe that we can receive as much as 74 gigabytes of information a day, yet our brain can only consciously handle 5-6 bytes per second (Heim S. and Keil A. 2017). This might imply that our subconscious is taking the brunt of the load and may still not be getting through everything. The sheer volume of information we take in every day is enormous and given that most of this information is designed to make us feel and think in certain ways, it is no wonder we get lost in it, feel overwhelmed, and lose touch with our sense of self.

Perhaps you have had the experience of feeling like there is not enough space to take everything in and process it, leaving you feeling like you lack time and are lost. When you look at these figures about how much information you are exposed to, then add in the other stuff of life that just happens, there are simply not enough seconds in the day to manage all the data being thrown at you and healthily integrate it. Your cognitive load refers to how much information you are holding in your working memory at any given time. Your allostatic load is the cumulative burden of chronic stress and life events (such as trauma, illness, and emotional distress). If cognitive load and allostatic load peak, you can be in trouble. When environmental challenges (external stresses you probably cannot control) exceed your ability to cope, then allostatic overload (internal distress) could ensue.

When your cognitive load reaches its limit through information saturation, this resource can then become depleted. Your allostatic load is then at risk of peaking from trauma or emotional stress because you cannot work through what has happened or process the feelings as there are little to no resources left to do this work. This combination of the allostatic and cognitive overload could push you into feeling overwhelmed, and subsequently becoming trapped in the fight, flight, or freeze responses. Once the allostatic load reaches its limit, it can lead to the chronification of illnesses (e.g., fatigue, migraines, pain), keeping you in a vicious cycle that is hard to break. You may experience emotional stress, activating your physical problems, and then your physical problems could worsen your emotional distress.

A good metaphor for this is when your computer or phone seems to stall. The app or program you are using freezes, and the dreaded 'wheel of death' starts spinning; it takes ages to work again. The device has too much going on, too much information to process. So, it must pause external operations until processing is finished. Your brain may work on a similar basis. Once your mind is full, the brain feels like it starts to slow down or freeze up. Your attention is difficult to maintain, and learning and understanding becomes much harder. You stall when you try to access your sense of self and accomplish things. This is particularly relevant in cases of trauma. When a trauma has not been fully processed or worked through, it can remain active as it has not been healthily integrated into the memory. This leads to unprocessed emotions being triggered, and our mental capacity and emotional availability are then dramatically reduced, which causes subsequent problems with our ability to function or manage any kind of work. We cannot focus on study, manage day-to-day life activities, it is harder to make decisions and our relationships are impacted.

Fortunately, just as our technological devices can be cleaned up by removing unnecessary files or programs, defragging and managed with firewalls, so, too, can our minds and our emotional bandwidth. If you actively engage with your sense of identity and take time to understand yourself better, you can start to gatekeep how much you take in and what you take on. You can select what you expose yourself to, what situations you become involved in. You can limit the risk of information saturation and reduce hyper-sensory experiences by taking respite moments to shut down and recoup energy. In doing so, you start to manage the input of information more actively and, therefore, create space to help with the processing of any trauma that you might have experienced and leaving you potentially freer to deal with those unexpected and distressing situations, supporting you to create and maintain your capacity levels. This is not necessarily a quick process, making lifestyle changes and feeling the benefits of these can take time, and you may choose to seek professional help to support you in processing heavy trauma.

It is important to acknowledge that life is never as easy as just saying, "I will change this," or "I will start doing that". For example, social media usage has been shown to directly increase neuroticism and anxiety. Yet many people simply cannot deactivate their accounts, which could possibly solve some of their anxiety. People know smoking is likely to give them lung cancer or other serious illnesses but cannot quit. A person in a domestic violence relationship may know they are being hurt and are in danger but does not leave. There are numerous examples of where humans can comprehend what is causing a problem but cannot action a solution. There are many reasons behind these blocks to changing and improving our lives, and it is important to not judge ourselves negatively as this won't help anything. We are complex beings, and our desire to try and simplify ourselves is unhelpful. Yet, we are understandably propelled into the desire for simplicity because life is full of complexity, 74 gigabytes a day worth of complexity!

It's All in Your Mind

The concept of 'mind' is something we still have limited knowledge about. The brain and mind are considered to carry out separate functions. The brain is an organ that manages the administrative business of the body, it looks after all the physical functions of the body like the co-ordination of movement and most of the body's organs are under its control. The mind, on the other hand, is not an organ and it tends to the management side of things. We do not know where the mind is located, yet it is one of the most intrinsically important components of who we are. Everything is channelled through the prism of our minds. Our minds generate our thoughts, choices and feelings. The mind manages our reasoning and understanding and our minds are not necessarily fixed. They can, under certain conditions, be changed, and when your mind changes, interestingly, so does the structure of your brain.

Dr Michael Gervais, a high-performance psychologist, describes three different "kinds of mind". He first discusses the negative mind, where our self-criticism, worry, doubt, and limiting thoughts make us feel like our minds are too busy. We can feel anxious and depressed and incapable of taking actions due to all the noise. It can be seen as a kind of cognitive collapse where our mind stalls, just like a computer that has too many programs open, demanding too much memory at once. This can also be referred to as our ego state, where we experience uncomfortable emotions and need external validation, labels or specific outcomes to know who we are. Once the ego achieves in one arena it may then move onto another, without necessarily taking time to appreciate accomplishments or recognise gains, potentially creating a pattern of dissatisfaction and unsustainable high demand. This negative mind becomes a fixed mind that stops us from feeling content, can keep us stuck in an always-wanting-more attitude, until eventually we are unable to move forward or integrate new information to support action.

The second kind of mind Dr Gervais describes is the "positive mind". This is where our optimism is, our hope. This is a place that creates space and support, where we actively encourage ourselves and access compassion to aid us in difficult moments. This is the growth mindset that can create and apply information to change ourselves and our life circumstances. The positive mind works with us to find solutions and uses understanding to promote commitment.

Finally, there is "no mind", a concept also held and taught within Buddhism and can be referred to as being in the awareness state. The business sector and extreme sports champions call this "a flow state" or "being in the zone". This is the space where you can make incredible achievements, find depths of inner peace, and increase creativity and learning capacity. It is where you are so present in the now that thoughts seem to fade away entirely. You operate on instinct, intuition and logic without conscious engagement of any of these abilities. When we are in the aware state, we can settle into an acceptance of "I am who I am", and this foundation gives us the stable base to see avenues for change and the capacity to sit with what cannot be changed, without fear, negative judgment, or self-deprecation.

One of Dr Gervais' most important reflections is that we cannot jump from the negative mind to the no mind. We cannot go from self-critical doubt and frustration straight to the potent and super capable arena of no mind. Unlike Monopoly, there is no direct route to go here. Both Dr Gervais and Buddhism recognise that we must **change our self-talk** from the unsustainable negative and critical to being calm and neutral, and, where possible, be positive. This can then allow us to be able to access the no mind or flow state, our super-charged awareness state, the most optimal state we can be in as humans - in other words, being out of our egos. In our egos, we can either be super-critical or over-inflate our abilities or our own importance. In the flow state, we create space where we can make choices consciously and carefully without a fixed identity. We can be just as we are.

In Buddhism, this requires us to renunciate or give up bad thoughts about ourselves, letting go of attachment to outcomes and turning towards who we really are. This can be achieved, in part, through the giving of love and compassion for the benefit of all, or, in other words, by being self-forgetful. To be able to achieve this, we must let go of any illusions we might have about the way things exist. This may mean challenging and changing our perceptions about who we are and what we need to be happy/successful/liked. For example, it might mean questioning the negative put-downs we say in our minds to ourselves, asking where do they come from, are they helping us or making us feel worse? It could run deeper and lead us to have to let go of ideals or dreams that have been very important to us, like we must have a child or have partner to be complete. Or, believing we must own a house to be considered successful, or that only by being the best at something can we be liked and respected.

Transferring from the negative mind to the positive or no mind is achieved by cultivating an understanding that we may not have or be these things, but we can still love our life. We can still be there for our family or friends. We can enjoy ourselves and not feel like we are missing out. It is not about denying that we might want these things, and there is nothing wrong in looking to achieve them. It is about developing a broader perspective that may help us feel more content, whatever the outcome. This shift in perspective could also reduce the chances of disappointment and help quieten self-critical thoughts.

We can look to see where the influence of the world or others is not helping us to achieve this broad acceptance of who we are. We might have been led to believe that we must have something to be complete, happy, and content, but that might not necessarily be true. We may have been made to feel we are not good enough from how we have been treated or what has happened to us. We may have developed an obligation to make everyone else feel happy, safe and satisfied at the expense of ourselves. We will be working gradually on all these areas across the 4 books, as just as there is not a direct path from the negative mind to the no mind state, there is no quick or straight path to changing how our minds have been working for years, possibly decades. The pathway to this calm, positive, and self-affirming mind where self-forgetting is used to make better choices for us and others can come with looking deeply at ourselves. Through introspection, we can find beliefs and behaviours that do not always support our best selves. The first segment of this work is about working out who you are and how you came to be this way. It is about **what helps you** and **what hinders you**. This is the fundamental first step to becoming psychodiverse, and thus able to use an adaptable and sustainable psychology to live your life from a space of proactively promoting and supporting your wellbeing.

Exercise: Self - Heredity - Cultural Identity

This exercise is about mapping out how you perceive yourself and what you know about you. It is designed to broaden your perspective to include the most influential aspects of your external world and how they impact your sense of who you are. You will need 3 big pieces of paper for this exercise, preferably at least A4 size.

Do not judge how much or how little you put down. Anything you put down is going to be useful. If you are struggling, come back to the exercise a few hours or even a few days later and try adding more components. Maybe ask other people you trust for their insights into who you are and how you behave. It might help to do this exercise with a professional therapist.

The idea is to spend a fair bit of time reflecting on what you know about you. Don't get caught up thinking it should look one way or another. There is no right or wrong way to do this exercise. Aim to fill up these bits of paper as much as you can. This map is our starting place for our work together and we will be coming back to this later to help guide us forward into feeling better and living better.

1. Copy the diagram below onto one piece of paper, then add in as many as possible of your:
   - Likes and dislikes
   - Things that you are afraid of
   - Negative, repetitive thoughts you have about yourself (e.g., I never get it right; I'm too fat; etc.)
   - Coping mechanisms for when you are stressed or in pain (e.g., talking to someone; drinking alcohol; etc.)
   - Personality traits (e.g., shy, introverted, loud, confident, etc.)

2. On a second piece of paper, repeat the same exercise for both your mother and father and/or the primary caregivers who raised you. You will probably have a lot less to put down for this part as you are only using your observations, and knowledge of others may be limited.

3. On your final piece of paper, please complete one for the culture/society that you were raised in and/or live in now. Think about what your culture approves and disapproves of. Add things that society values (e.g., wealth, kindness, status). Think about the kinds of programs you watch or podcasts you listen to. What themes do you spot in them? What are the morals, ethics and values shown through them? What do the adverts in your world try to sell you?

We will use these maps throughout all four books to help you reflect on how you see yourself and support you in identifying where certain patterns of behaviour may have originated. The purpose of examining the behaviours and personalities of your

3. You Do You.

parents or caregivers—as well as the influence of your society and culture—is to provide insight into how your ways of being, coping, and expressing your personality may have been shaped. Please note, this is not about attributing blame, but rather about gaining understanding. Knowing where something has come from can help you decide whether it's something you wish to keep or let go of.

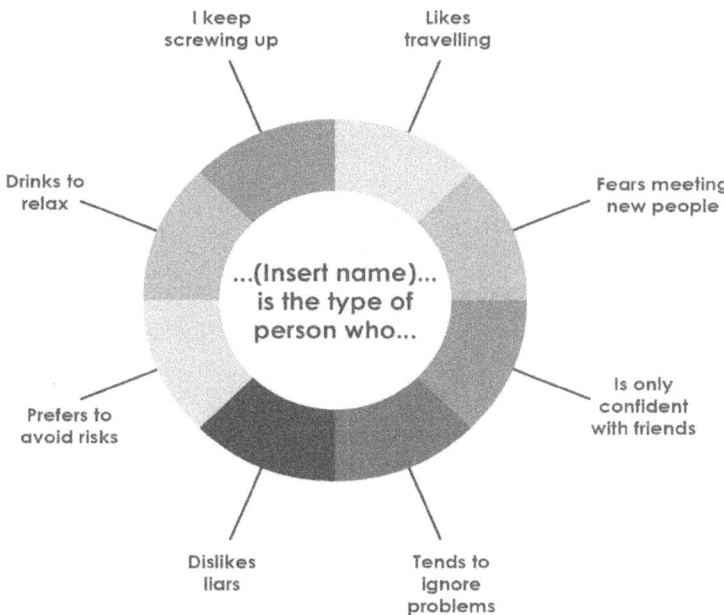

If you find this exercise brings up difficult emotions, please pause and consider seeking support from a therapist or mental health professional.

Pause—Reflect—Landscape

1. Pause - Take a moment to sit with what you have just learned and consider it.

- Gathering information on ourselves and actively choosing what we get exposed to may help us manage finite resources, reduce risks, make safer choices, and protect ourselves, by knowing what works for us and what doesn't.
- It is helpful to see all aspects of ourselves, not just one part of our identity.
- Over exposure to information and stimulation may affect our mental and emotional capacities.
- If we hit our cognitive and emotional overload, our brains can stall and we move into fight, flight and freeze modes, potentially becoming stuck there and this could create other health problems for us.
- It is helpful to manage our exposure to the unrelenting flow of information we are bombarded with today, and create space to process emotional experiences to avoid feeling overwhelmed and falling too regularly into the fight, flight or freeze state.

3. You Do You.

- The negative mind is self-critical, anxious, limiting and does not assist us to move towards solutions. The positive mind gives us hope, support and encouragement towards growth. The no mind state allows us to make seemingly effortless achievements, access creativity and find deep inner peace.
- We need to first foster a positive mind space to be able to then access the super effective, creative, productive and easeful no-mind state, and we can aid this process by giving up and letting go of negative thoughts.

2. Reflect – Looking at what you have learned, and using your identity maps that show you how you see yourself, reflect on the following:

- What can you see in your maps that is working for you? Is there anything in there that is harming you now or could hurt you in the future?
- Is your mind a negative mind, a positive mind or have you noticed that at times you can move into the no mind state?
- Can you recognise any ideas or beliefs you have about yourself that have been influenced by experiences, other people or the media?

3. Landscape - Take a step back to see how this new information fits in with the bigger picture of your life. Consider your history, what is going on for you now, who and what is in your life, and the future you want for yourself.

- ✓ How much information are you exposed to every day? Is there an excess of stimulation in your life?
- ✓ Where could you make changes to lessen you mental and emotional load? Are there any blocks to doing this?
- ✓ What aspects of your personality could assist you in adapting your mind from the negative to the positive?

4.
Getting to You: A Map for the Voyage

In this section you will be learning about:

- → How our brain is communicating with our body.
- → How our core values and beliefs may shape our behaviour and feelings.
- → Why repetition matters for change to be successful.
- → How changing our experiences in life may be achieved by changing our perceptions.
- → How to use our strengths to support and manage our vulnerabilities.

You will need:

- ✓ Pen and paper to take note of insights and carry out an exercise.
- ✓ Your identity maps from chapter 3.
- ✓ To be open to discussing your reactions, feelings, and ideas, either with yourself or others.

4. Getting to You: A Map for the Voyage

"Beliefs are not the thing. They are the results of your journey."

R.J. Blizzard

Most of us have, at some point, wanted to change a feeling or a behaviour. We either want to start doing something or stop doing something. Or we want to change how we are feeling. It might be that, despite our best efforts, we sometimes return to familiar patterns or the previous status quo. For example, we stop going to the gym or start smoking again. We replace anger with happiness only to feel angry again the next day. For many people, this scenario of creating fleeting, unsustainable change is all too familiar, and the search for a lasting solution continues, usually with the realisation that somehow will power alone is not enough.

Cognitive-reprogramming is a technique that can help us in making changes that could assist with altering both our behaviour and emotional experience. It provides us with the ability to go beyond will power into a space where repetitive changes can be used to help support the potential for building new neural pathways. Research suggests that our thoughts are closely linked with activity in the brain that can influence the release of neurotransmitters and hormones.

These chemical messengers can impact how we feel, behave, and physically respond to situations. For example, recurring or intense thoughts may activate brain regions involved in emotion, stress, or motivation, such as the amygdala or hypothalamus, leading to shifts in our emotions or changes in our behaviour. While this process is complex and not always linear, it highlights the connection between what we think, how we act, and how we feel. This understanding forms the basis of many cognitive and behavioural approaches to mental health, which suggest that by becoming more aware of our thought patterns, and gently challenging the unhelpful ones, we may be able to influence our behaviours and emotional experiences in supportive ways.

But where exactly do thoughts come from, what generates or influences our thinking? Do they just appear in our mind or is there a basis for them? Thoughts can be generated from our core beliefs and values, and whilst our core beliefs and values are formed across our lives, we adopt most of them in our early years, when our brains are first forming and downloading information from our environment. Beliefs and values can come from our family of origin, our educational system, our society and culture, a religion or spiritual faith. When asked how to define a belief, many will simply say it is something you believe in. A closer look at a belief might reveal that it is something you believe to be true. Another way of looking at it is that beliefs are just thoughts you keep thinking. Think something long enough, often enough and with trust that it must be true, and you may end up believing it. What this means for creating sustainable change is that reframing your thoughts alone is not necessarily going to be enough. Our core beliefs and core values could potentially influence multiple

4. Getting to You: A Map for the Voyage

thought streams, in which case they may also need altering to support longer-term changes in how we think, feel, or respond to challenges.

Human behaviour is driven by both our conscious and unconscious (or automatic) practices. The conscious mind allows us to reflect, plan, and make intentional choices, while many of our routines, reactions, and learned patterns operate outside of conscious awareness. Researchers suggest that a significant portion of our daily actions are influenced by the automatic practices developed through a combination of repetition and early experiences. These patterns, often called habits, could be beneficial to us, but as we know some habits can be unhelpful, and some could even be harmful. While exact estimates vary, some studies indicate that our unconscious practices guide a large amount of our daily behaviour. That is, you are not actively thinking about how you act, nor choosing to act consciously. If some of our less helpful habits are stored in or driven by our unconscious it is going to be much harder to identify them and make changes. This can help explain why change is sometimes challenging and frustrating, especially if we rely only on willpower.

The good news is we can use our biology to support us in making changes. This is because, once we have repeated a behaviour or belief sufficiently over time, we can strengthen neural pathways in the brain, making those responses more automatic. This means that, with consistent repetition, some behaviours may begin to feel more easeful or require less conscious effort, occurring more naturally and spontaneously. Changing behaviour in the long-term with will power alone can be very hard. The reason being for this is when our attention is not sufficiently focused on changing, our autopilot (unconscious) mind can revert to familiar patterns that have been reinforced over time. That's why building supportive habits gradually, with awareness and repetition, can be more effective than relying on motivation or effort alone.

Conveniently, the same processes that help form unhelpful beliefs may also support us in gradually adjusting them. **When we identify core beliefs that are contributing to unhelpful thinking, we can begin to explore supportive and more balanced alternatives.** With active awareness and consistent repetition our new thoughts, in time, may influence how we feel and behave. For example, you may value kindness and believe you must put others' needs above your own, but this sometimes can lead to burnout and leave you with insufficient resources left to care well for yourself. By retaining the value of kindness and expanding this to include valuing self-kindness, and moderating your belief to balance putting the needs of others as equal to your own, you create space for more sustainable wellbeing. With ongoing awareness and practice, the adjusted belief can align more closely with your values, supporting you to make choices that nurture both yourself and your relationships.

This example might help to demonstrate how this process works to help you connect with the science. As a teenager, I don't fit neatly into any kind of group. I am not in the popular group. I am not sporty. Picture the kid who never got picked for the teams; that's me. I am not smart enough to be with the nerds, and I don't connect with the alternative group either. Essentially, I simply don't fit in anywhere, which leads me to feeling like I do not belong, and therefore, I feel that I am not good enough. Then smoking comes along. Smoking requires little talent or skill, so it is something I can manage. Plus,

4. Getting to You: A Map for the Voyage

all the cool people in the media smoke. Thus, by joining the smoking group, I connect with all kinds of people: the popular people, the sporty people, even the artsy people. Finally, I belong. I am a smoker, with the vague hope of looking as cool as all those people in the media do. Thus, I feel good enough when I smoke.

Having a sense of belonging is something most of us want to have and we all want to experience the feeling of being good enough. When we find a behaviour that generates these feelings, we are going to trying to repeat that behaviour as much as possible. So, after a while, I can come up with 15 to 20 reasons to smoke a cigarette every day: I'm bored, so I'll have a cigarette; I'm stressed, so I'll have a cigarette; I finished my meal, so I'll have a cigarette; I had an argument with my boyfriend, so I'll have a cigarette. You get the idea. This repetitive behaviour starts to build and reinforce the belief that smoking helps me belong and feel good enough, as science tells us, neurons that fire together wire together. So, the more this behaviour and feeling gets repeated, the more likely it becomes a habit, and it starts to sit in the unconscious part of my mind.

Essentially, and putting it simplistically, the belief that I am not good enough and wanting to belong is generating thoughts in my mind that are then driving my behaviour to smoke a cigarette and making me feel better. When I am reaching for a cigarette, my body is not communicating back to me that this might cause cancer or that is costing me a lot of money. My body cannot distinguish this is bad for me. The moment I started smoking, I feel like I belong to a group, so I feel good enough. Over time and with lots of repetition this creates a core belief that smoking helps me feel like I belong, and with every subsequent cigarette I smoke this repetition is further reinforced and the belief moves deeper into my unconscious mind. Smoking helps me feel good enough. Overtime, this connection of belonging and feeling good enough to smoking is lost to the unconscious and I become unaware that this is why I need to smoke.

As I get older, I learn more and consciously accept that smoking really isn't good for my health, and it does cost a lot of money. So, I try to quit. I work hard on not reaching for the cigarettes when I am in a traffic jam. I stop drinking coffee to avoid wanting a cigarette with it, and I cope with the cravings. Then one night, I am out after a bad day at work and at home, I am feeling that I am not good enough and my attention is somewhere else, so old habits take over. When my friend offers me a cigarette, I accept and start to feel better. Then, suddenly, a short while later, I remember, oh that's right, I quit.

When I finally come around to successfully stopping smoking many years later, before I even cut back on how many cigarettes I smoke a day, I spend between 6 and 12 months just thinking about how much I do not like smoking. I become much more aware about how it makes my body feel, what it could do to my body long-term, and how much it costs me. I focus on how smoking really makes me feel: the nausea, the discomfort in my lungs, and the way I am so quickly out of breath from only walking up short staircases. I start to think I do not want to belong to the smoker's group. I want to belong with others who value their health, and because of this I start to feel that I am not good enough when I am smoking.

This allows me to start gradually changing my fundamental belief that smoking helps me belong and feel good enough. I know I don't want to fit in with people by doing something that is going to hurt me or compromise me financially. So,

I choose to fit in with people who look after their bodies. I invest time and energy in exercising, in understanding nutrition better, and shifting my focus to connect with people who care about how they look after their bodies. Smoking no longer helps me feel I belong or good enough. Thus, eventually, I can cease smoking, and, hopefully, I am developing a healthier, more sustainable lifestyle. I no longer believe that smoking helps me feel that I belong, and I now feel good enough from making better choices that will serve my wellbeing on the long-term.

Understanding how our core beliefs and core values influence our behaviour and feelings is the starting point for a more in-depth awareness of ourselves and what works for us and what does not. We can start by tracking how our negative thoughts lead us into actions that harm or hurt us. From here, we can then look to see if they are unhelpful beliefs that are driving these behaviours. This way, when we think negatively, destructively, and hopelessly, we can start to recognise where these thoughts come from, and be more selective around how we engage with them.

Reconnaissance of the Self

Let's return for a moment to a previous analogy. Elite forces will not carry out a mission without first seeking out intelligence regarding the situation that they will be facing: the terrain, the resources they have, political allies involved, etc. Reconnaissance work will be undertaken first. From this information, strategies and plans are used to manage, mitigate, and counter any foreseeable issues. Tackling change within yourself is much the same. You need to gather intelligence on what your strengths are, your areas of vulnerability, and any unhelpful habits that might cost you allies that could help you. For this to happen, first you need to be honest with yourself about your unsupportive habits and negative thinking patterns. Some of this might be challenging and even painful to look at. So, before working with those vulnerabilities or less helpful habits, let's start with your strengths.

Our strengths are what **pull us through** challenges and help us modify behaviours that we need to address. Be careful not to become attached to the idea that your strengths are external assets or resources. We are talking internal strengths here, not whether you have financial means or know all the right people. An internal strength might be that, despite facing constant challenges, you are still looking for a way to help yourself. You are still seeking answers or change. This shows your commitment to yourself, a capacity for resilience and faith. At the end of the day when you feel at your worst, it is not the person with all the awards and the latest fashions that you seek, it is the person who does not give up, who keeps moving forward with encouragement, and who has hope of something better. You may need to dig into yourself for your internal strengths. They might not be immediately obvious, but they are there.

Our strengths can be used to help support us in facing our vulnerabilities and tackling unhelpful behaviours that we might have been repeating for decades. They can lead the way and support us through confidence or self-belief that we can move towards a process of change. Our strengths quite literally make us feel strong. They make us feel good about ourselves. From this place of positivity and acceptance of what we can do well and recognising these positive attributes we possess, it is

4. Getting to You: A Map for the Voyage

much easier to deal with the less helpful habits that we can all have from time to time.

Sometimes, new strengths may be found in transferable skills. For example, perhaps you are very good at caring for other people and helping them to feel more positive when they are down; this is a strength. You can use this same skill to encourage yourself and be kind, after you make a mistake or when you do something very human that you initially judge yourself for harshly, or to change an old belief that you'll never be good enough. If you do a job such as accounting and have an eye for spotting details that could create problems if not adjusted, you can use this to look at your own behaviour in relationships. It could, for example, allow you to spot when you are saying things in a way that causes the other person to move into reactivity. A slight adjustment of the wording or tone could make a vast difference to how your communication gets received.

Finding techniques to change the harmful aspects of our behaviour or the ways in which we manage the hurt from negative experiences requires some experimentation. Some techniques will work better than others. One size does not fit all in the case of psychological and emotional management. By reflecting on your strengths and drawing on them for courage and willingness, you may begin to identify unhelpful habits, underlying beliefs, or conflicting values. From there, you can explore different ways to support your brain in forming more helpful habits, ones that may aid in coping with discomfort and building self-belief over time. The fact you are reading this book is already a strength. It shows you are open to learning and changing through being present and curious, and that is a good start.

Exercise: Strengths Supporting Vulnerabilities

1. Take some time now to write down as many of your strengths as you can. You can use your identify map from chapter 3 to help you with this. This might be hard at first, but it is important you do this and find as many as possible.

   If you are struggling to identify your strengths, think about people you respect and admire and identify their strengths. Ask yourself if you have anything in common with them in this regard, for example, you might admire a football player who is dedicated to their training and you too are dedicated to something in your life, whether it is a job, study, a person etc.

   Look at things you feel passionate about - there may be some clues in there too. You might value protecting animals, which shows your kindness and compassion, these are both strengths. Maybe you have some people you trust and can ask them what they think your strengths are.

2. Next, see if you can write out your values, you can also use your identity map from chapter 3 to help with this. Some may be more obvious than others, for example you have written down you like to be around considerate people, this would indicate you value kindness. Some may be less obvious, you may have written down you fear the unknown, this

4. Getting to You: A Map for the Voyage

could indicate you value information and being prepared. Identifying your values can be tough, but stick with and it and maybe ask someone else or a professional to help if you get stuck.

3. Then, using your identity map from chapter 3, look at the negative things you have written down about yourself.

   It might be things you do that you don't like. It might be feeling a certain way about yourself or just feeling a particular way all the time that causes you problems, like being anxious. It might be that you have some unhelpful or harmful coping skills such as avoiding problems.

   Once you have isolated them all, see if there are any common themes or beliefs that sit behind them. For example, does not liking the way you look mean you believe you are not good enough? Or that you keep making mistakes indicates you put yourself under too much pressure because you believe you have to be perfect?

4. Finally, look back at your strengths and see if there are any assets that you could use to help with changing the negative beliefs and behaviours that harm you, or managing the values that contradict with your beliefs. For example, you are passionate about music, could you source this passion at social functions where there is music in the background to help you feel more confident when socialising? Can your caring nature be directed at encouraging you to say nicer things to yourself when stuff goes wrong, as you know you can be too hard on yourself.

If you find this exercise brings up difficult emotions, please pause and consider seeking support from a therapist or mental health professional.

Pause—Reflect—Landscape

1. Pause - Take a moment to sit with what you have just learned and consider it.

- Our beliefs can generate our thoughts. Thoughts can drive our behaviour. Behaviours may elicit emotional responses. These emotions may feedback to reinforce the original belief.

- We operate either through conscious or unconscious processes, and much of our daily life is driven from the unconscious and automatic parts of our brain.

- Neuroscience tells us that repeated behaviours can strengthen neural pathways, making them more automatic over time, and potentially place them into the unconscious.

- Habits can feel hard to break, even when our conscious mind knows they're no longer serving us.

- Cognitive-reprogramming may support us in changing our behaviour and altering feelings.

- Beliefs are just thoughts we keep thinking. Not all our beliefs help us, some may be unhelpful and some may harm us.

- Sometimes our beliefs and values contradict each other, and this could cause us to mismanage our own wellbeing.
- Changing our beliefs may assist us in developing more supportive habits.
- Our strengths can help in supporting us to changing negative beliefs and caretake our vulnerabilities.

2. Reflect – Looking at what you have learned, and your strengths, your beliefs and values, and the negative ways you have of treating yourself, reflect on the following:

- What qualities and strengths do I have that can help me manage change and challenges better?
- What habits do I have that help me?
- What do I do to myself that hurts or harms me?

3. Landscape - Take a step back to see how this new information fits in with the bigger picture of your life. Consider your history, what is going on for you now, who and what is in your life, and the future you want for yourself.

- ✓ Do I have any beliefs and values that clash, contradict each other or can lead to depleting my resources?
- ✓ Where do the negative habits I have that hurt me come from? Who or what has led me to believe this is an OK way to treat myself?
- ✓ If I start to change some of the negative things I do or say to myself, is that going to change any of my existing relationships? Is that a good thing or a bad thing?

5.
Consciousness: Ego vs Awareness

In this section you will be learning about:

- → What our consciousness is.
- → How the ego behaves and what our awareness can do.
- → How to use giving and receiving compassion to access our awareness.

You will need:

- ✓ A focus on compassion as a gateway to awareness.
- ✓ To be willing to identify your own ego-based beliefs and behaviours.
- ✓ Pen and paper to make notes on insights.
- ✓ A quiet place and time to meditate.
- ✓ To be open to discussing your reactions, feelings, and ideas, either with yourself or others.

5. Consciousness: Ego vs Awareness

"The moment you become aware of the ego in you, it is strictly speaking no longer the ego, but just an old, conditioned mind-pattern. Ego implies unawareness. Awareness and ego cannot coexist."

Eckhart Tolle

Consciousness is the totality of experience that a person is aware of at any one moment. It can be perceived through two channels, our ego or our awareness. The ego relates to our perceived external identity, it is focused on what we are doing, what we have, and our fears for the future. It can help us work out who we are by sometimes showing us who we are not, or rather how we do not want to feel. When operating from the ego part of our consciousness, we are more likely to experience uncomfortable emotional states, feel lost and unhappy, bored, anxious and more stressed. The ego that remains unchecked may create problems for us and others.

The ego consciousness is always trying to work out who it is from the outside in. It wants an identity. Thus, it will define itself by activity, by material possessions, and by achievements. This, in turn, can restrict us from seeing the bigger picture of who we are. The ego never allows you to see yourself as a whole. For example, the ego says, "I'm overweight," a sentiment that is typically laden with negative feelings and judgment. Regardless of whether you have gained weight, it has no bearing on the kind of person you are, how hard you work, or how much you care for others. The ego completely ignores the fact that slight weight gain does not equal anything bad and does not make you ugly. Nor does the ego recognise that, even if you have gained weight to an unhealthy degree, you can also lose it. The ego does not acknowledge that others like us for who we are, not our size, shape, or weight. Generally speaking, at funerals, people do not reflect on how thin someone was, but rather on the kindnesses they showed, or their sense of humour. The ego mind is based in fear and a lack mentality, it strives to be separate, which can make you feel disconnected as a result.

Awareness is the state of consciousness where we may feel full of contentment, where we are likely to be at peace with who we are and can access more compassion, potentially leading us to feel more connected to ourselves and others. It is the more positive side of our consciousness. When in this part of our self, we may feel happier with who we are. We have less need to define ourselves through job titles or achievements. We can more easily just be and accept who we are in any given moment. We don't even need to make a social media post about it.

When operating from within the awareness consciousness, we can increase our chances to make more responsive decisions, with a readiness to accept all possible outcomes and have faith in our abilities to cope, no matter what happens. In the ego state, we can act out of fear and limitation, and make impulsive, less considered, or reactive choices. This is because, when in the ego, we select to do something on the basis of thinking "without this or that" we will be less, and our ego always wants more. Thus, we can become fixated on one outcome and laden the process with expectations that may not be able to be met, for various reasons that are most likely beyond our control. When the outcome our ego desires is not achieved, the ego often shifts into a limited viewpoint. It may decide it is all our fault (even when it is not) or not our fault (even when it might be). From there, the ego can spiral into the belief that we are not good enough or simply unlucky.

In awareness, you are more able to choose something from a place of completion, of knowing you are already fine just the way you are, and trusting that you will cope with any outcome, and then you can more effectively manage any unhelpful expectations and assumptions. This means you may be less impacted by disappointment, and you may be able to support yourself into feeling content and at peace, no matter what the outcome. In the aware state it can be easier to identify any negative thoughts we have about ourselves, and then we can start to unravel what we believe regarding our own worth and what we may or may not deserve. From this compassionate and gentle space of awareness, we can start to understand why we do certain things in the way that we do. We can start to see which beliefs help us and which ones can harm us.

For example, we smoke cigarettes even though we know that they can damage our physical health. Yet we continue to smoke, and repeated attempts to quit are thwarted. If we can see that we started smoking to fit in socially with our peers, allowing us to feel good enough, then we could also see that we believe smoking helps us to feel like we belong and that we are enough, but that this is an ego belief as it is based on an external event occurring, i.e. smoking. And even in seeing that smoking can cause us harm, our ego can prefer to access the feeling of being good enough and belonging by smoking, over protecting our long-term physical and financial health. The ego's need for validation by others overrides the need for long-term health and security. Our awareness will see that there is not much point belonging if we get sick, have no money to meet up with others, or worst-case scenario end up with a terminal illness from smoking. Thus, our awareness can reshuffle our priorities to match our deeper values around spending time connecting with people and steer us towards being around those who do not smoke, and learning to feel good enough without taking particular actions, becoming satisfied and comfortable to be ourselves.

This kind of ego-limited view can appear in all sorts of scenarios where we are doing something that is probably hurting us, yet we persist in doing it, such as being in a dangerous relationship, eating unhealthily, not exercising, or staying in a job that is making us stressed and sick. Working through our awareness, we can re-assess our priorities in terms of our beliefs and values, and possibly see how they can contradict one another and cause us internal conflict. Whilst this is a complex process, by getting to the bottom of it we can gradually make changes to support our wellbeing. For example, if you feel that you need a drink to socialise and this evolves over time into you becoming a heavy regular drinker, your future health is at risk. Your awareness and ego can collaborate to show you the drinking is an issue, but the underlying problem is you are feeling insecure, and you worry that people won't like you unless you have a few drinks on board, as you are then more confident and funnier. This insight into the deeper issue allows you to move more from your awareness state, which may assist you in taking a more compassionate and broader view of your internal perception. This could help you notice that you have other likable qualities and attributes that people can engage with, outside of the effects of alcohol, and assist you in seeing that you would like to be connected with people not only because they think you are confident and funny, but also because they see you are kind, a good conversationalist and have lived an interesting life.

Whilst the ego is a tricky thing to deal with, our egos are there for a reason. They provide us with balance and insight by showing us what works and what does not. By knowing who we are not, we can know who we are. Your ego can give you boundaries, short-term confidence, and signs when something deeper inside might be amiss. Taming the ego is a skill that requires ongoing practice, and we all fall into our egos at some point or another. Don't judge the "judging ego". Move straight back to awareness by accepting it as a facet of being human, and use it to aid you in adapting and sustaining a healthier awareness-based state of being.

Focusing on **giving and receiving compassion** is a good place to start accessing and using your awareness. When we are in this place of compassion, we are automatically in our awareness. From this clearer space, we may look at things we are feeling conflicted about and we might find it easier to make decisions that could serve our best interests in both the short and long-term. For example, we might truly value having a relationship and someone to love, but this value is keeping us in an unhealthy relationship. Or we may want to stop drinking but have previously believed that consuming more alcohol was a sign of how strong we are. So, ceasing to drink would clash with this previously held belief and may make us think we are weak and thus feel bad about ourselves. Fortunately, as our beliefs are just thoughts we keep thinking, beliefs can, therefore, be changed by thinking new thoughts. By altering our beliefs, we can move more easily into a place of awareness, rather than ego, and gently support ourselves in changing behaviour that is harming us, without the negativity and judgment of the ego getting in the way. For example, by changing your belief that how much you drink is a measure of how good you are, to measuring your worth through other actions and attributes, you can enjoy less alcohol without feeling weak or less than. You could change your belief, so that you feel acceptable and capable whether you have partner or not, then you can leave an unhealthy relationship and be comfortable being alone whilst you look for a better one.

Compassion may also help manage the kind of ego-based thinking that can trip us up in our relationships. For example, our ego may put in a boundary to protect us with someone who has activated our triggers by making the other person feel bad for doing so, and then when we trigger the other person and they try to push back and make us feel bad, our ego reacts, saying they cannot bring their issues into the relationship. Potentially, creating an unhealthy imbalance. This may lead to a scenario where our understanding only seems to run one way and creates a feeling for the other person that we are being hypocritical, wanting their care and consideration but not having to provide it back. Compassion may help ameliorate the ego out of the picture, so we can still put in a boundary, but with kindness and presence, and when we trigger someone else, this same compassion shows us how to support them and the experiences that they have been affected by.

Our ego and awareness play important roles in balancing our consciousness and capacity to grow and be content. Too much ego, and we can lose the appreciation of what it is just to be. Too little ego, we can lose motivation and the drive to fulfil more of our potential. Too much ego and the need for the self to have an identity and achieve more can become detrimental, not only to ourselves but to those around us. Our awareness can be the balance to our ego. If the ego is all about the self and achieving, then to step into our awareness we can focus on others and just being content with what we have or who we are. It is through compassion that we can achieve this balanced ego, through compassion for ourselves and compassion for others. Compassion can be the gateway that allows us to let go of identities, achievements, labels, outcomes and just accept what is and work towards collective benefits.

Exercise: Creating a Compassionate Breathwork

Compassion is not necessarily a natural or easy state for us to move into and finding ways in which to practice accessing compassion for yourself and others can help you tame and balance the ego, so that it serves you well rather than gets in your way.

This is a simple guided meditation designed to help you access your compassion for yourself and others. If it resonates with you, practice it every day, even in the simplest of ways. Placing a hand on your arm offers self-comfort during a difficult moment—a gentle acknowledgement of another's troubles, with a kind tone, supportive words and when appropriate a soft touch. Look to find small ways to create moments of compassion every day. This exercise is also available to listen to on our website.

- Find yourself a comfortable position. This can be seated or lying down. It needs to be one you can stay in for a while without needing to adjust. Either close your eyes or hold a soft gaze. Gently place your hand on a part of your body that feels comfortable and reassuring to you.

- Use the sense of touch to connect to your awareness and bring in kindness and softness towards yourself. Now bring your awareness to the breath. Start to shape your breath by making it a bit longer and deeper.

5. Consciousness: Ego vs Awareness

- Connect to the feeling of life that breathing brings with each inhale, and the release and relaxation of each exhale. Find a comfortable way to breathe that allows you to feel at ease.

- Continue to witness your breath smoothly entering and filling the body, drawing your awareness to the soft air moving into your body, and soothing you from the inside.

- Breathing slower and deeper, take your time just to breathe. When you draw your breath in, imagine that the air is full of kindness, that the air is gently easing away any tension and stress.

- As you inhale, add in whatever quality you feel you need at this time: love, compassion, a sense of being held or cared for. Focus on the feeling of this quality or call to mind an image of what it might look like to you.

- Then move your awareness to your exhaling breath. Feel the air soothe you as you breathe out. Notice how the exhaling breath allows you to feel even more relaxed.

- Think of someone or something that is important to you. It might be someone who is close to you or an issue in the world that needs peace around it. Hold the image clearly in your mind. Then as you exhale, imagine that the soothing energy of the out-breath flowing towards that person or situation you are thinking of. Send them compassion, kindness, and ease.

- As you breathe in, the energy of compassion flows toward you. As you breathe out, the energy of compassion flows to those you care for. Feel that graceful flow of drawing in the energy for you and sending it out to others, balancing the compassion between yourself and others. As ocean waves rise and fall, so does your breath, ebbing and flowing as if it were the most natural movement in the world.

- Bring your awareness back to the breath. Let go any of shaping of the breath, any shaping of your imagination or your intention, and just be as you are, in a state of gentle and complete self-acceptance.

Pause — Reflect — Landscape

1. Pause - Take a moment to sit with what you have just learned and consider it.

- Consciousness is how much we are able to be present in any given moment.

- The ego state relies on an identity and is rarely satisfied for long. It is more a singularly focused state and may use unhelpful comparisons of activity, material possessions and achievements as measures for success and worth. The ego can keep us trapped in unhealthy patterns and situations. Our ego can, also at times, be a motivating force that helps us seek out or take up new opportunities that lead to growth and creativity.

- Awareness is our more contented state, where we may find peace with who and what we are and what we have. It has more opportunity to take in the breadth of all our identities and capacities to be able to accept "I am who I am", without needing to be like others. It may support us into more balanced decisions and assist in setting us up for accepting outcomes, with less reliance on the "must have" or an "I need" attitude, that can lead to or amplify feelings of failure disappointment and hurt.

- Identifying our conflicting beliefs and values that prevent or block positive change can aid in helping us move into a state of awareness, which may then help us change our circumstances.

- By learning how to temper our ego with our awareness, to know when we have enough or done enough, we may be able to source confidence from the ego to handle challenges or achieve goals.

- Giving and receiving compassion may support us in mediating our ability to oscillate between the ego and awareness and remain balanced in our consciousness.

2. Reflect – Looking at what you have learned, and what you know about yourself, reflect on the following:

- What is my understanding of what is ego-based behaviour and awareness-based behaviour? What might show me I am in my ego versus being in a more aware state?

- Can I see times when I have acted from my ego and times when I have been in my awareness? Are there things I can do from my ego state that harm me or hurt others?

3. Landscape - Take a step back to see how this new information fits in with the bigger picture of your life. Consider your history, what is going on for you now, who and what is in your life, and the future you want for yourself.

- ✓ Do I know how it feels to show compassion to myself or others? Where in my life do I show myself and others compassion? Is this something I need to do more of?

5. Consciousness: Ego vs Awareness

- ✓ How has my ego shown up for me in the past? Is it present through certain habits now? Can I see my ego in the ways I treat people or my relationships?
- ✓ Can I think I am being aware and yet still be caught up in my ego? Are there times I have made one rule or standard for me, but another for other people? In what ways can my ego sneak in and take over and make me think I am aware when I am not?

6.
Assumption is a Poor Currency

In this section you will be learning about:

- → How we can fool ourselves.
- → What are the risks of too much faking it and not enough making it.
- → How being 'ok to be you' can lead to increasing psychodiversity.
- → Why we self-sabotage.
- → How self-compassion can aid us in being ok with things we find hard about ourselves.

You will need:

- ✓ A gentle and understanding attitude towards yourself.
- ✓ A quiet space and time to do a breathing exercise and meditate on yourself.
- ✓ Be ready to reflect on what you know about you and what might not be true.
- ✓ Pen and paper to take note of insights.
- ✓ To be open to discussing your reactions, feelings, and ideas, either with yourself or others.

6. Assumption is a Poor Currency

"Begin challenging your own assumptions. Your assumptions are your windows on the world. Scrub them off every once in while, or the light won't come in."

Alan Alda

Make sure you have your identity maps from Chapter 3 handy and have a look over them before reading this chapter. They may be helpful in revealing what kind of person you think you are and where you have been influenced by experiences, people and the media. Remember to bring a nonjudgmental and compassionate attitude to any insights. This work is not about apportioning blame, nor holding anything against ourselves or sitting in anger, it is about understanding who we are and why we became this way from a place of gentle acceptance and awareness that change is possible. The next step is to start working out what ideas you have about yourself that do not work for you. Do your beliefs enrich your life? Do any thoughts you have about who you are hold you back? Did you create any to keep yourself safe from being hurt? Which of these ideas been given to you by others? What you do next with this information is as important as having it. Now you will begin to work out what is really true to your core nature (who we are on a instinctual or heart level) and what has been influenced, affected, or created, either by others or from your experiences. Assuming what you think you know to be true about you is risky because it very well might not be the truth. It might be a subtle injury of influence.

Knowing the difference between awareness and ego can help us navigate through what is useful in our collection of beliefs and help us see what needs to be altered. To do this, we need to know if we are deceiving ourselves into believing that we are something that we are not. This work must be approached with care, especially if we have formulated ways of protecting ourselves through certain types of negative beliefs, trying not to attract to much attention, trying to not be better than anyone else or believing we are not worth anything so no one will come near us, and thus keep us safe from any kind of harm. Believing bad things about ourselves may put significant limits on or even blocks to our personal growth. For example, if you keep saying you cannot cope with change, then you may become the person who cannot cope with change, but this might not be who you are all the time. Or sometimes, we convince ourselves we are OK with something bad that has happened, but our behaviour indicates we are very far from being truly OK. Another example could be by assuming and stating that we are an anxious person, because we have had experiences of anxiety, we may risk locking ourselves inside an uncomfortable emotional experience, making it unhelpfully, and inaccurately, part of our personality. Humans can have an unfortunate habit of believing everything they think is true. We do not always question our minds often enough, especially when it comes to that negative mind and self-critical voice. By not questioning our assumptions about ourselves, we may cause ourselves problems, both in the moment and later.

Have you heard of the 'fake it till you make it' or the

6. Assumption is a Poor Currency

manifesting what you want type of thinking? It's generally about creating what you want in your life by acting as if you already have it. This may work for our feelings, like acting confident, acting gracious, and acting brave enough to take chances. But when it comes to defining ourselves, or claiming something is fixed when our actions indicate otherwise, we may risk moving from pretence to self-deception. What happens when faking it until you make it just stays at faking it? There are many reasons people pretend something is ok when it is not, it is one of those things that all humans can do, so do not bring in any harsh criticism or judgment. We may fear what speaking the truth might mean, for ourselves and for others. Everyone can develop blind spots, believing they are right, that the other is wrong, that they have developed a skill perfectly, or that they are superior to others for some reason. We might defend someone as a good person despite the fact they are doing bad things, maybe because we want to see the best in them, we don't want to be wrong about them, or we don't want to let them go. These are all fairly common behaviours, and we probably all develop some kind of blind spot at some point in our lives. The danger comes from repeating the assumption, pretence, or self-deception because repetition could wire it into our brains and we risk it becoming an unconscious process. Then distinguishing what we believe to be true from what is happening or who we are may become difficult. Then we may risk repeating mistakes.

Imposter syndrome is a good example of an assumption gone wrong. It is loosely defined as feeling like a fraud and doubting your abilities. It is commonly seen in high-achieving people. They are unable to acknowledge their own accomplishments. Those with this syndrome question whether they have earned or deserve accolades and/or compliments. This is a fear-based syndrome that sits in the realm of the ego. Typically, people engage with this kind of imposter thinking if they are already insecure or they have been exposed to gaslighting or some other form of emotional or psychological manipulation that has made them feel to blame for something that is not their fault or made to doubt themselves. It can come from being overexposed to the influence of advertisements that make you constantly feel inferior because of how you look, where you live, or what you can or cannot do. Imposter syndrome can be toxic and distracting and may create or worsen self-doubt, or lead to avoidance of taking opportunities and induce self-sabotaging behaviours. It is an issue to gently address and care for through the compassionate redirection of negative thinking towards yourself. It may be something you seek professional help with.

In Western life, our identity often hinges on how we curate our online persona or our external image. This is the self that people see more than they get to know. We may deliberately create and project images of ourselves as how we want others to perceive us. This might be done through social media platforms or how we physically look or through our external achievements. You may have noticed that rarely does anyone post a video of themselves having a big meltdown, or of their children running riot in the house, or failing to win an award, or having that inevitable bad hair day. This could become unhealthy because we might convince ourselves that our lives have to be perfect, and that we have to be perfect. Or we can risk seeing ourselves unrealistically or believing our work is done, or that we are complete/perfected. We may start to fear we will never live up to the all the other perfect

6. Assumption is a Poor Currency

peoples' lives we see online. Working on yourself in the context of developing your own adaptable sustainable psychology is a process that is not intended to be finite with a clear end. In this space, it is about working on accepting that we are always growing and changing, without the pressure for perfectionism or notion of completion.

If the focus is only on how you are perceived, you may not be considering how you are received. Receiving is the space in which you affect, impact and connect with others. It is how others feel you and how they feel about you. If your investment with how you look to others overshadows how you make people feel about you, then your collective development or collective awareness could be limited and potentially harmful to yourself and other people. Your relationships maybe superficial or short lived, you may unintentionally hurt people or cause unhealthy comparisons. This kind of "I am all done and perfected" attitude can lead to an individual being unaware of things that hurt or derail others through their behaviours. It is even possible the individual who thinks they are done and living their best life can get in their own way of balanced contentment. This person may experience behind-the-scenes breakdowns that they hide from everyone. Or maybe drink their way through their problems whilst attesting publicly about their healthy lifestyle. This then creates separate public and private faces. One might be the opposite of the other, creating an emotional disharmony that leads to discomfort from within. The shame of the not-so-perfect self leads to hiding it from others and eventually even yourself, and what is hidden and denied cannot be helped and healed. It is completely ok to care about how you appear to others, just be mindful that your inner landscape and how you are received is given as much attention, love and support.

Become a Thinking Wizard!

Metacognition is thinking about our own thinking. This is an opportunity to understand ourselves at the deepest level. It is in this arena that we may be able to identify if we are pretending to others and/or deceiving ourselves. It is here that we can see if we are masking any fear of being hurt or shame that we may have in confronting the things we do not like about ourselves or reluctance in dealing with the things we are doing that are not serving ourselves or others, or where we may be judging ourselves unfairly or overly harshly. Self-deception can easily become self-sabotage, a state where we either consciously or unconsciously set ourselves on a course of action that will result in failure. This might be due to us fearing success or fearing people will pay us more attention if we do well. It can be the fear that we can't succeed, so it is quicker and easier to fail, or we assume we don't deserve to succeed. There could be many reasons, and this may be an area to discuss with a professional therapist. When self-sabotaging behaviour remains unchecked, it can lead to stalling or even a complete breakdown, which then fuels the self-saboteur to feel even worse about themselves.

We are inevitably our own worst critics. By being harsh towards ourselves or by using violent language inside our minds, we may block opportunities for change and growth. Remember that there is no direct pathway from the self-critical judge to "no mind", the state in which we can achieve at our best. A more sustainable route that moves us away from pretending, assuming, or self-deceiving via a self-critical narrative in our heads to being positive and supportive is found through the skill of self-compassion. Learning to provide ourselves with compassion is one of the greatest challenges some of us face.

Many do not know where to even start. This is especially true if you carry any kind of trauma where you have been assaulted, violated, or hurt in a way that has led you to think you do not deserve to be respected, cared for, or honoured.

One of the simplest ways to learn about self-compassion is to **care for yourself as you would care for a child or loved one**. You would make sure they were well-fed with healthy foods. You would encourage them to be fit and active, help them to do the things they enjoy doing, ensure they get plenty of rest, and facilitate opportunities to be social. Perhaps most importantly, you would comfort and positively encourage them when they are feeling down or when something has not worked out the way they had hoped. You would reassure them when they made a mistake that these things happen, gently encourage them to forgive themselves and remind them we can always learn something. Self-care is not necessarily limited to spending money, drinking with mates, or making yourself look your best. It is also about being kind to yourself in both how your mind talks to you and the actions you take to look after yourself. Be your own compassionate self-coach.

The information you are starting to unravel about your identity is worth questioning. Have you assumed it is all accurate? Could you have got some off those negative beliefs or views about yourself wrong? Perhaps you used them to keep yourself safe, but now they are doing more harm than good. Is there any chance you are pretending or deceiving yourself? Do your actions really match your words? Would other people truly confirm your self-perception? Moving towards an honest, open, balanced, and broad perception of who you are and how you move through the world is the foundation for building your psychodiversity. A distorted self-perception ultimately may become unsustainable and could make it harder to adapt and grow. It helps to master being self-compassionate to resolve any assumptions you have made about yourself that are not fair or soften any expectations that put you under too much pressure. It is with self-compassion you can see if there is an unhelpful assumption or pretence, self-deceit, or self-sabotage lurking anywhere in your patterns. Use kind, gentle understanding to see that this is how humans who have been hurt, negatively influenced, or mistreated act and comfort yourself that these are things that can be changed, whether you seek any extra help or ask a professional to assist. Once you can own it, you can grow, and then you can start seeing yourself beyond these fears and hurts and change that which does not serve or suit you.

Exercise: Just Being - Breathing Meditation

This exercise may offer support in recognising unhelpful assumptions or noticing moments when you might be pretending, sabotaging, or being unkind to yourself. Approaching these patterns with self-compassion could assist in making adjustments that feel healthier for you. By practicing understanding and honesty with yourself, you may find it easier to acknowledge challenges without as much fear of judgment. This can open a space for you to actively take ownership of what feels important to address in your life.

The act of self-compassion may support you when coming to face those difficult things about yourself or the experiences that you have been exposed to. This gentle breathing exercise is a good place to start, and it can be a technique you can come back to in difficult moments to help ground, calm, and comfort yourself in an unobtrusive and easy manner. This exercise is available to listen to on our website.

- Find yourself a comfortable position. This can be seated or lying down. It needs to be one you can stay in for a while without needing to adjust. Either close your eyes or hold a soft gaze.

- Gently place your hand on a part of your body that feels comfortable and reassuring to you. Use the sense of touch to connect to your awareness and bring in kindness and softness towards yourself.

- Start to shape your breath by slowing it down, making the inhaling and exhaling breath just that touch deeper and longer. Imagine the breath filling you up to the crown of your head as you breathe in. As you breathe out, feel the air washing down to the tip of your toes, like a wave of breath washing up and down your entire body.

- Take time now to be with your breath, feeling your ribcage fill and your stomach rise as the air fills your body, and feel the body softly sinking deeper towards the ground as you exhale out all the air in your body.

- Bring your awareness inwards with a soft and kind attitude. Find gentleness through your breath towards your mind and body.

- If your mind drifts off into thought, simply acknowledge this has happened, then gently bring yourself back to your breath.

- Now release any shaping of your breath and simply let your body breathe you.

- Observe the rise and fall of the body just as the ocean ebbs and flows on the shore. Feel each wave of breath moving in and out of your body, up and down from the crown of the head to the tip of the toes.

- Allow yourself to be as you are. Allow the breath to guide you into the present moment and being ok just as you.

6. Assumption is a Poor Currency

- Bring yourself back into the room, back to your body.
- Slowly and gently open your eyes.

Pause—Reflect—Landscape

1. Pause - Take a moment to sit with what you have just learned and consider it.

- Assuming negative beliefs about us are true could be unhelpful, potentially harmful and unsustainable.
- If we deceive ourselves by either believing a negative or positive attribute that isn't true, we could limit our capacity to change or overcome challenges.
- It's important to compassionately question the validity of the assumptions we have about ourselves, as faking it or imposter syndrome can disguise deep held insecurities and self-doubt, which could be softened and changed using our awareness to adjust core beliefs and values that do not serve us.
- How we are received by others is more important than how we are perceived.
- Thinking about our thinking may show us where assumptions have led to pretence or self-deception and hidden fears and doubts from us.
- Self-deception can lead to self-sabotage but could be supported towards change with self-compassion, and

by caring for ourselves as we would a loved one, by encouraging self-acceptance through altering negative behaviours not serving us.

2. Reflect – Looking at what you have learned, and what you know about yourself, reflect on the following:

- Do you believe something about yourself that might not be true and could harm you or others?
- Do your assumptions turn into pretending with others or lead to sabotaging yourself?
- Do you worry more about how people see you, rather than how they receive your behaviour?

3. Landscape - Take a step back to see how this new information fits in with the bigger picture of your life. Consider your history, what is going on for you now, who and what is in your life, and the future you want for yourself.

- ✓ Are there any people, outside influences or experiences in your life that have led you to feel you need to pretend that you are something you are not? Would you consider seeking professional help to heal these? Or address them with self-compassion and evolving kinder ways to see yourself?
- ✓ Are there areas of your life, or relationships, that will be changed if you release negative beliefs about yourself or if you stop acting a certain way? Could this release free you to explore more ways of being in the world, and improve your life on the longer term?

- ✓ Do you see times when you thought you had it all sorted and then it turns out you didn't? Are you at risk from this kind of thinking in the future? Can you embrace the value of a constantly evolving process to learn and grow?

7.

The Illusion of Self-Phobia: A Close and Personal Danger

In this section you will be learning about:

- → How we can be afraid of ourselves.
- → Why illusions may get a hold of our sense of self.
- → The difference between relative truths and absolute truths.
- → How we might access our expectations to expose our fears and illusions.

You will need:

- ✓ Time to connect to yourself to practice using your behaviour, feelings and body sensations to guide you into your thoughts and beliefs.
- ✓ To be aware that we briefly discuss childhood trauma, so remember to check-in and identify if you feel ready to engage with this area.
- ✓ Pen and paper to do a written exercise.
- ✓ To be open to discussing your reactions, feelings, and ideas either with yourself or others.

7. The Illusion of Self-Phobia: A Close and Personal Danger

"The greatest enemy of progress is the illusion of knowledge."

John Young

You are hopefully starting to see some underlying themes from the exercises we have done about how you see yourself. There might be some insights emerging about how you value yourself, what you recognise as strengths and what you judge as weaknesses. Perhaps you have observed that you can be somewhat unfairly harsh or critical of yourself. You may not feel good enough or worthy.

Self-phobia is a fear of oneself. It comes from having a fear of who you are and thinking you do not possess the capacity to change. Essentially, it is the sense that you cannot cope and can lead you to find ways to not have to face coping. Self-phobia can also be about having a fear of being with yourself because you fear what you might feel or see, particularly in the absence of activity or other people to distract you from yourself. This can lead to constant busyness and distraction becoming your daily habit, maybe getting you to the point where you cannot enjoy your own company and have an inability to be comfortable with yourself. Self-phobia can involve self-loathing and a background of high, often unrealistic expectations. You can develop a belief that you are not good enough that has nothing to do with reality, which, in turn gives you the illusion of feeling unworthy. An illusion that can all feel too real.

Creating illusions is a skill many of our brains have. An illusion is an instance of a wrong or misinterpreted perception of a sensory experience. The optical illusions created using geometric shapes to distort our senses were very popular a while back. Our brain would see something 3-dimensional in a 2-dimensional picture. We can all make illusions and sometimes they can be fun and quirky and sometimes they can be deeply unhelpful and possibly even frightening. Anyone with a trauma background will know how their brain can take a sensory experience from the trauma and overlay this into the present moment, making the person fully believe they are once again at risk. This brings with it all the feelings, fears, and bodily responses as if it were entirely real. Our brains are incredible. They can completely convince us something innocuous can be dangerous or that something utterly dreadful is acceptable, such as any form of criminal violence.

Let me give you a gentle example of a fear-fuelled illusion. One day in my therapy room, I was coming to the end of a session with a client when I observed a small-ish spider dangling on a thread about 2-feet away from my client. As the session was almost over, I decided it was best not to risk scaring the client, and to wait until they left to deal with the spider. I could keep an eye on it, and if it did move, I could then ask the client to move. The spider spun on its thread and seemed to get bigger from different angles as the session came to a close, and I became more nervous, as I have a fear of spiders. The moment the client left, I raced out the room to grab

7. The Illusion of Self-Phobia: A Close and Personal Danger

the insect spray and self-coached myself to not be afraid, that I could do this, and to take a deep breath. I returned ready to battle with the 1-inch spider that was hanging above my couch, only to realise it was a starfish shape bead on a decorative thread that hung from my ceiling. I would have sworn in any court of law that the starfish bead was a spider. My brain had made an illusion that was not real, yet my fear and anxiety had been very real.

If we are only using how other people treat us as the marker and evidence for the type of person that we are, we are likely to end up feeling bad about ourselves. People can be insecure, hurt, and frightened. They can be careless and inconsiderate and they can carry unresolved wounds and can make choices that hurt others unintentionally, especially during childhood. Some can treat other people badly to either distract themselves from their own pain, or make themselves feel less lonely by making someone else seem as bad as they are. Or they may even want to make themselves feel better by putting someone else down. When taking ideas about our identity from people who mistreat us, we risk self-creating an illusion that can lead us to think the worst of ourselves because we think we must be truly bad for people to treat us that badly. This is particularly true in childhood trauma. At an early age, a child cannot realise someone is committing a crime by subjecting them to abuse, the child may assume they must a terrible person for this person to hurt them this way, they may presume it must be a punishment for some wrongdoing. Because, they have been taught, typically, if they are good, they are rewarded, and as the abuse is so horrible and they cannot find an action they have done wrong, they may deduce it must be them who is inherently bad. It can also be a mechanism for survival, by thinking you are not good enough and constantly feeling ashamed this may help protect you from the further harm from your abuser. Unfortunately, this way of thinking may get layered into the brain from an early age and is then at risk of being repeated, especially when anything else goes wrong or someone else mistreats you later, it can result in forming a key dynamic for mis-assessing self-worth. "When people treat me badly, it's my fault for being a bad person, I deserve it."

Some possibly helpful ways to reframe this equation, where you assess your own worth based on people's treatment of you, is to consider if you would not seek out and ask the advice of the person who is mistreating you, why would you believe what they say about you? Is it helpful to form an opinion of yourself based on how their abuse makes you feel? Do you think that you might be better off forming your opinion of yourself based on your own actions. How do you treat others? Do you offer compassion, understanding, and kindness to people? Do you show up for others in need? Do you work or study hard? Do you try to be considerate and contribute? Maybe your actions show a decent and considerate human being who has a lot to offer. Not someone, who is bad and worthless.

By looking at how you move through the world, the things you say, the actions you take, how you treat other people, etc., you are more likely to get a fair gauge of the type of person you are. Once aware of our negative illusions about ourselves and we recognise how this makes us feel, we can re-direct the illusion into an opinion that is based on our all our different identities and our thoughts and actions, an opinion which is therefore much more likely to be supportive, nurturing, and kind. The more we repeat this kind of reflection, of basing our view of who we are against our choices, actions and intentions,

7. The Illusion of Self-Phobia: A Close and Personal Danger

then there is a greater chance of this becoming our normal, everyday unconscious process of kindlier self-reflection. Potentially reducing self-phobia and maybe increasing our capacity to be softer with our expectations on ourselves.

Real, or not Real?

Our dreams are a terrific example of how the brain cannot always distinguish between real and not real. All you need to do is recall a time when you have awoken from a dream, good or bad, and felt the emotions associated with that dream. Perhaps you have woken with your heart racing or even felt out of breath or have been punching the air. The brain does not always distinguish between something that is happening only in our minds and not occurring in the physical world. If our brain thinks about it, then the brain can send the chemistry, aka signals, to our physical body and create the actions and stimulate the emotions appropriate to what our brain is thinking/dreaming about.

A useful example of navigating between real and not real experiences is in the fictional story of *The Hunger Games* by Suzanne Collins. After the character, Peta, is kidnapped and exposed to mind conditioning using hallucinogens and gaslighting, he cannot distinguish between what are his actual memories and what has been manipulated. He asks the protagonist, Katniss, periodically if his thoughts and memories are real or not real for validation. Anyone who has been exposed to gaslighting, be it from an intimate partner, manager, family member, or friend will know how hard it is to work out if something is true or not. Gaslighting is a type of emotional and psychological manipulation that is focused on trying to make someone question their own sense of reality. The one doing the gaslighting may feel better about themselves through making someone else look less than them in some way or they could need to feel like they have control in such a situation. The insecure and vulnerable person that questions themselves, has a tendency to blame themselves or believe they are not worth much is potentially more susceptible to this kind of manipulation. As those who gaslight can more easily access control through someone's insecurities and self-doubts, and they may use this to their advantage. Protecting your self-worth might help insulate you and reduce the risks of gaslighting and manipulation being used against you.

In some ways, advertisers, popular media and news broadcasts, and politicians can operate through a similar principle of manipulation. They can seek out our fears and insecurities and play on these in order to get us to buy their products and services, watch their shows or support their campaign. There are other types of illusions that are softer, perhaps less dangerous and more subtle, such as marketers or social media influencers who may try to show us what kind of life and experience, we could have by using certain products and services. They can hire out expensive houses and lots of beautiful people as a backdrop for a product to create the illusion that if you too use this product, you may look popular, rich or feel stylish. They can act based on a premise that we are all the same. They might demonstrate a type of product that will never work the same on someone older or younger etc., but the assumption promoted is that this product could do for you what it does for them, regardless of differences. It is all an illusion. It is all a manipulation designed to use our insecurities for gain, and not necessarily about our best interests.

7. The Illusion of Self-Phobia: A Close and Personal Danger

Two Types of Truth

So how do we navigate what is true and what is an illusion? There are **two types of truth** in our world: **relative truth** and **absolute truth**. An easy way to understand the difference between these two types of truth is to use the example of the rising sun. Most people would automatically declare this an absolute truth, as the sun absolutely rises every morning. However, if you were to leave planet Earth and watch the sun from outer space you would observe that the sun neither rises nor falls. It simply remains where it is and planet Earth orbits around the sun spinning on its axis. Thus, it gives the illusion of a sun rising and falling, making it a relative truth that the sun rises, relative to you being on planet Earth. There are likely very few absolute truths in our universe.

What does this imply about what you believe to be true about you? Look back over your work so far. What are the things that you believe to be true about you that are not kind, that are negative, based on past experiences or beliefs given to you by others? Are there things you think are true, but have come from someone who used you in order to feel better about themselves, who hurt you and needed you to take the blame to avoid their own guilt, or simply to sell you a product so they could make money? Is it possible that these are not absolute truths about you? Could they be illusions given to you by the actions or opinions of others, and not based your own behaviour or nature?

The Reality of Expectations

Expectations are a good window into understanding our fears and illusions. An expectation is a bit like an illusion or fear, it is not founded in absolute certainty or truth, but we can believe that it is. They are typically created through a combination of our past, our fears for the future, and our beliefs about life, ourselves, and others. Expectations are typically followed by a strong emotional experience. This **emotion is a cue** that you can use to find out what your original expectation is and, more importantly, what beliefs are sitting behind it. You can then ascertain if the beliefs are helping or hindering you. Think of your emotions as an alarm system telling you that something is up, and it needs your attention.

Expectations are not about reality, but they are an illusion we have about a possible reality. They are about what we think will or will not happen and we can create emotional outcomes accordingly. Perhaps think about a recent time when you have been frustrated, the feeling of frustration is the cue, now what was behind that feeling? Was there an expectation that did or did not get met? Here is an example to help you. You set off to drive to work at your usual time only to encounter roadworks, and therefore arrive late. You are angry and frustrated at the delay. You expected to drive to work as normal with no issues. You had not foreseen any delays, and had not allowed additional time. The reason you feel frustrated at this expectation not being met comes from how your late arrival might be perceived or judged. You fear being judged for being late or getting told off. The idea of being a bad person or seen as not being good enough by arriving late comes from societal influence and prior experiences. Perhaps you had parents that told you it was bad manners to be late. Or you went to a school that punished you with detentions for being late. So, you learned to value punctuality and reliability, but you fear punishment and/or being rejected for failing to arrive on time.

7. The Illusion of Self-Phobia: A Close and Personal Danger

Arriving late also makes you feel guilty, and you worry you will be perceived as not being capable or good enough by others. So, now you are feeling angry at the traffic, frustrated at being late, guilty for letting others down, ashamed that you are not living up to expectations, and fearful of being in trouble. All this is from an expectation of having a clear run to work and being able to arrive on time.

The hidden or underlying belief sitting under this expectation is about you being good enough by being perfect, and the need to get it right all the time, which is fairly unrealistic and unfair on yourself. We can look to alter this belief, and accept that nothing (most likely) has gone drastically wrong from our lateness, that it doesn't make us less of a person if occasionally we make a mistake. You are still good enough even when late, as being on time isn't integral to your entire skillset or capacity. Then you could maybe continue your day without feeling angry, frustrated, guilty, and ashamed, making it a much more pleasant day. You could even use it as a positive learning opportunity that always leaving an extra 5-10 minutes early might prevent the issue from recurring, too.

Exercise: Know Your Expectations

Use the diagram below to help you cultivate the ability to understand what your expectations are in any given situation. You will not need to list all of your expectations. Start with one or two, and start to get a feel for the exercise, then consciously engage with the process during day-to-day life anytime a strong emotion arises, investigate to see what lies beneath it, and this may help you resolve uncomfortable emotions more quickly and kindly. Once again, the more you practice the process the greater chance you have of making it an automatic response that can activate to help you negotiate and manage uncomfortable or overwhelming emotions

The idea is to get you used to this way of looking beyond your feelings and reactions to find out *if* there is an unhelpful or unfair belief behind the expectation. Then you can alter the belief driving the expectation, so you can operate from a place of self-compassion, kindness, understanding, and adaptive learning.

This exercise is designed to help you develop other ways of managing your thinking. Instead of simply being in the feelings and then repeating the process time after time, you can start to learn how to dismantle your feelings and understand yourself better. You can see where you have some untrue or

7. The Illusion of Self-Phobia: A Close and Personal Danger

unfair illusions about yourself or maybe others. In doing this, you can examine how helpful your ideas are and see if they make you feel at ease within yourself, or if they are creating a sense of dis-ease.

Often by just changing your approach to your thinking, you can move yourself out of those uncomfortable feelings into a more peaceful space, one that maybe does not fatigue you as much, (because feeling uncomfortable emotions is tiring), and one that might support you to make decisions that hopefully do not create other problems for you.

Work through each of the questions in the diagram below using a recent memory where you had a reasonably strong emotional reaction. Maybe pick a low to medium situation as your starting point to get a feel for the exercise before progressing to the bigger emotional experiences. An example of how the process can work is given in the second part of the diagram to help guide you.

If you find this exercise brings up difficult emotions, please pause and consider seeking support from a therapist or mental health professional.

Questions:

What are you feeling?	What is the situation you are in?	Did you have an expectation about this situation?
Are there beliefs connected to this feeling?	Does this trigger any new feeling(s)?	Do you know where that expectation has come from?
Where have these beliefs come from?	Are they fair and reasonable beliefs?	What are the consequences of keeping the beliefs?

Example Answers:

Shock	My partner just left me	We would always be together
I am not worth it, no one will want me	Betrayed, foolish, not good enough	Relationships work for other people
Other similar experiences	No, there might be someone who will stay with me	I will be afraid to try again and be alone

Pause—Reflect—Landscape

1. Pause - Take a moment to sit with what you have just learned and consider it.

- Self-phobia is fear of oneself and thinking we cannot change; it can be covered up by always being busy or with others. It can involve self-loathing and the setting up of unrealistic expectations on oneself and a feeling of not being good enough.
- Minds can create illusions, and they can be generated through fears and past traumas.
- Using how other people have treated us to measure our worth could be fraught with problems and likely to end up creating unfair and untrue beliefs about ourselves. We might be better off assessing who we are based on our actions and the way we treat others.
- A relative truth is based only on the information available, previous experiences or certain conditions being met, and therefore subject to change. An absolute truth means it is true in all situations possible, all the time.
- At times we can believe everything that we think about is an absolute truth and this may not be the case. Questioning if something is going to be true in every situation, and will always be true every time, can

help establish if what we believe is a relative truth or absolute truth.

- Our minds cannot always distinguish between what is happening in the external world and an illusion we experience. We may need to seek out the difference between absolute and relative truths before forming an opinion or taking action.

- Our emotions are a cue that something might need our attention, and our expectations are a window into our beliefs.

- This process of using emotions as an alert to find the expectation and identify the belief behind it may help guide us into reformulating any potentially unhelpful illusions and beliefs.

2. Reflect – Looking at what you have learned, and what you know about yourself, reflect on the following:

- Do you avoid being with yourself? Do you always keep busy, or can you sit quietly with yourself?

- Are the negative things you believe about yourself relative to either your prior experiences or what others have told you about yourself? Or are they absolute truths that cannot be disproved in any circumstance and can never change? *For example, you believe you are weak, but this was due to an experience you could not prevent when you were a child and an overbearing boss who told you that when you asked for time off. This would be a relative truth, relative to your experience and what your boss said. You could be strong in many other areas of your life and can say no to things you don't want to do because you're an adult*

7. The Illusion of Self-Phobia: A Close and Personal Danger

> *now, and you can improve your strength with support and practice, therefore "I am weak" cannot be absolutely true.*

- Do you put pressure on yourself to achieve high expectations, or do you have tendencies towards being a perfectionist? How do you feel about challenging and changing some of your expectations?

3. **Landscape** - Take a step back to see how this new information fits in with the bigger picture of your life. Consider your history, what is going on for you now, who and what is in your life, and the future you want for yourself.

- ✓ When you look back over the course of your life, how much do you think your opinion of yourself has been guided or influenced by other people, experiences or the media? Is any of this affecting how you live your life, or could it damage you later? How does believing a negative opinion of yourself make you feel? What could be the value in reassessing negative beliefs about yourself, are there any potential payoffs?
- ✓ How much of your life and how you have managed difficult events has been affected by having high or unrealistic expectations? Did having these expectations shield you from discomfort or pain or expose you to more problems because they created an illusion that ultimately could not match reality?
- ✓ What are the negatives and positives that could come from changing your expectations? Are there fears that if you alter your expectations others will take advantage of you? Or are you concerned that you won't push yourself to do better?

8.
Being an Emotional Alchemist

In this section you will be learning about:

- → Why we think delays in decision-making are unhelpful and how we could make them useful.
- → What motivates us to be unmotivated.
- → How self-judgment blocks self-evolution.
- → How to practice tuning in and out of ourselves to help manage our minds better.

You will need:

- ✓ A piece of music or song that has several different instruments that you can listen to.
- ✓ Pen and paper to make notes on any insights.
- ✓ A quiet place and time to conduct a meditation.
- ✓ To be open to discussing your reactions, feelings, and ideas either with yourself or others.

8. Being an Emotional Alchemist

An old alchemist gave the following consolation to one of his disciples: "No matter how isolated you are and how lonely you feel, if you do your work truly and conscientiously, unknown friends will come and seek you."

Carl Jung

Our feelings are normal, natural and, most of the time, probably completely fair and understandable given the situation we are in. But this does not mean they are always comfortable, and if left unattended, they can become unhelpful or disproportionate to the situation. Working out how to move from one emotional state to another, transforming your emotional experiences into something supportive and constructive, is what emotional alchemy is all about. It is a skill we are not always intuitively connected to, and when we are dealing with stronger, more intense emotional experiences, we may have to apply more mindful awareness and patience into the process of being that emotional alchemist. Sometimes, it is the conflicting emotions that are the most damaging and difficult to deal with. Our emotions can be pulling us in different directions that contradict one another, and this may impact or reduce our capacity to feel motivated and able to act. For example, excitement and dread can both come from a promising job offer, one with a good salary but demanding aspects. We might feel both warm anticipation and anxiety over a hot date, feeling excited about the potential but worrying that it might not go anywhere. When we can't work out the direction our emotions are guiding us and we start to move into feeling overwhelmed by this confusion we can become indecisive, and eventually, ambivalent. Then we may be stuck and not moving at all and the driving force to do anything has gone.

But this is not the only thinking net that we can get caught in. There's also procrastination. Whilst they produce similar results, feeling demotivated, getting stuck and being unable to act, they operate using different mechanisms. The phrase "when in doubt, don't," can be a useful pause button to hit when an answer to our situation is not clear. It can allow time for more information to surface or a clearer insight to appear into what we actually want to be gained. However, when we are not consciously interacting with our indecision and tapping into what this might be showing us, we may move into ambivalence and become motionless. This is not necessarily a comfortable emotional space to hold, and it can trigger other aspects of our self-doubt and disable our capacity for motivation from the internal conflict that is pulling us in different directions and usurping our energy resources. We then risk spiralling into anxious and depressed states. Ambivalence can be a dangerous and difficult space to be in, especially when we have conflicting needs that override one another, as they could keep us trapped in unhealthy behaviours or dangerous situations that may eventually move us into overwhelm. Being ambivalent can potentially drain our finite mental and emotional resources as we try to manage the incompatible parts of ourselves. Trying to unravel ambivalence is tricky when you do

8. Being an Emotional Alchemist

not fully know yourself, when you are not comfortable with who you are, and you are not consciously engaging with your values and actively tying them to your situation and decisions.

Navigating through ambivalence might be assisted by viewing the situation through the lens of our ego and awareness. When we sit in ego, we can focus on the external and the image being created for others to perceive and may be tying our ability to feel good to a specific outcome. We might care more about what other people think rather than what we think, and we may not see past a particular outcome for other opportunities to be happy and content. This could lead us into behaviours and decisions that do not serve us, but instead make us look a certain way to the outside world or keep us rigidly focused on one outcome. For example, we may stay with a bad spouse because we fear being alone and do not want to be divorced and seen as socially unacceptable. We might not want to stop drinking as all our friends do, and we fear they won't understand, then we may have no friends left. Ambivalence could stop us from seeing we could find a better spouse in the future or be happy single, it might not see that new friends who choose not drink could come into our lives through the new pastimes we take up. We can't see possibility and therefore we find it harder to feel motivated to take any kind of action.

Taking your ambivalence and turning it into something useful requires the support of your awareness, as awareness can open you up to potential alternate pathways and provide you with the hope of possible opportunities, which in turn may restore your motivation. The ego can show you what core beliefs or values are getting in the way through the narrowed and limited actions and outcomes it gives you. In the examples above, the ego is saying you will only get or must only have one spouse, and you believe you can't make new friends. In awareness, you can recognise that you are feeling ambivalent and why, without negatively judging it. You are unhappy in your marriage, but your values contradict you leaving, and you fear being negatively judged as a divorcee, doubting that you are good enough, unless you are in a relationship. Your awareness state can support you in accepting what is happening without judging it, and may help identify the root causes of your ambivalence. It could, for example, help you reflect that you were raised to believe you only marry once, that you had no luck dating prior to getting married and fear you are too old to meet anyone new. You could then use this information to understand yourself better without negative judgments getting in the way, and be more compassionate about your ambivalence to see how you have become caught between your unsatisfactory present and your beliefs and values.

When you have this information about the conflicting parts of yourself, you can return to your base values and core beliefs to work out a path forward. Returning to our earlier example, whilst you value being in a relationship, you see that you also do not believe you should be treated badly. In the ego state you focus on the label and identity of being in a relationship, the self-doubt that you are not good enough and the fear that you wouldn't find another partner and will have no financial support, all of which can override the importance of how you are being treated. With awareness, you may see that your beliefs and values have come from an outdated societal judgment you do not wish to be part of, that you are now older and able to see where your dating in the past went wrong and thus, you may now feel able to make better choices, you know how to be happy in yourself as you have already been doing this

8. Being an Emotional Alchemist

whilst living inside a bad marriage anyway and you may then feel motivated to make the decision that you would rather find ways to cope financially and trust in yourself, than be abused and unhappy. Thus, you resolve the ambivalence by choosing how you are treated and feeling over the outdated values and unhelpful beliefs, so that you can leave the bad relationship.

This is a very simplified example, and there are often many reasons people cannot leave relationships, but you get the idea of how your ego can limit you and keep you in ambivalence. Awareness, however, can start to free you to see the bigger picture and support you in managing any blocks or resistance to making decisions. Using information gained through the lens of your awareness could help you unravel the ambivalence, and help you identify if you need to be willing to take **a short-term loss to achieve a long-term gain**. Getting rid of the unhealthy relationship might hurt initially and cause you stress, but it could free you to find a kind one, and whilst having less money or finding a new home is hard, so is living in unhappiness and pain every day. Both pathways take energy and have risks, but one path (leaving) is more likely to end up in a place of safety, while the other path (staying) leads to more pain.

Negatively judging your ambivalence is unhelpful. Try to find what will serve you best in the bigger picture. Usually, we are in ambivalence due to a cost-benefit-analysis scenario, where we are weighing up options in the limited ego state that is fuelled by fear and self-doubt. When we open inwards our awareness lets us see where our situation sits in relation to our core beliefs and values, and how they could be preventing us from acting in our own best interests. As core beliefs and values can be altered it means we can make more informed choices, we choose what to keep and what to change to serve us best now, and the long-term, and thus we transform stagnation into movement. In awareness, we become an emotional alchemist, turning information into support and direction.

In ASP terms, this is where your psychodiversity can play a helpful role in supporting you out of ambivalence. By using different techniques, such as self-compassion, identity mapping and focusing on your strengths, you can engage with your beliefs and values, identifying what you see yourself as being capable of or what you doubt you can do and move towards adjusting these accordingly. Knowing that we can change the beliefs that do not serve us can provide hope and inspiration for a new direction, both of which feed our motivation. You can then work out what needs to change in order for your situation to become a better fit for you in the short and the long-term, consciously choosing to match your actions to support your new beliefs and move towards your goals. You then may adapt accordingly, and have more capacity for creating a sustainable, safe path for your future self. ASP is about being the **psychological opportunist** that can respond to situations in whatever way might be most effective at the time, as well as being beneficial later on.

When we are comfortable resting in a space of "I am who I am" and can be ok with that, then we are less inclined and perhaps feel less pressured to feed the ego's need for attention, labels, outcomes and validation, and we can move towards gradually changing unhelpful beliefs or alter values that no longer suit our circumstances. We may provide validation to ourselves instead, a potentially much more beneficial tonic, and we can adapt our beliefs to support our safety and well-being, softening feelings of overwhelm with supported decision-making that aligns to who we are, not what society or events have shaped us into. Providing ourselves with approval can be worth more than the value of someone else giving it to us and sometimes our evolution is about subtle shifts in core values to help us recognise our wellbeing and happiness is as important as anyone else's. We can access ways to assist in the reduction or prevalence of ambivalence, and create space and support for choices that can align well with who we are, the stage of life we are in, where we are headed, and the type of life we wish to continue to live.

The Human Doth Procrastinate Too Much

Procrastination is the action of delaying or postponing something. It has had a bit of bad rap over the years, being seen as a negative trait. But as you are learning, how we view and perceive emotions, behaviours and habits can dictate their utility or their futility. Procrastination can follow ambivalence and take the contradictory feelings beyond stagnation into a freeze state, where even the negative consequences of delaying are insufficient to prompt action, there is no space left at all for motivation as the fear of the wrong choice completely blocks it. For example, we may need to quit our job because we are so stressed we are becoming sick, but we like the people we work with and the next job might be no better, and we fear losing our job security having been with this employer so long. So, we hesitate, frozen and continually questioning risks and benefits, all the while getting more stressed and sicker. However, procrastination can also be a useful option when people need to deliberately delay a decision in order to be sure of covering all contingencies or see if new information or if other options arise, or because they do better when they have fewer resources available and are under pressure. Procrastination can have some difficult consequences, and it can be a useful strategy. If you are aware that you can procrastinate and unsure if it is bad habit, once again, maybe go back to "if in doubt, don't." That pause button is a useful tool that we can make the most of by choosing not to negatively judge our habit of procrastinating.

Whether we are judging ourselves or someone else, we're applying internal pressure to hurry up and decide and that is not helpful. This could make decision-making a more stressful process than it needs to be. Finding the balance between enough pause and enough processing towards action can prevent us from sinking into a quagmire of negative delay and minimise negative consequences. Buying yourself time to procrastinate and decide to act or not could at times be an advantage. Circumstances can change suddenly to be more favourable than they were. You might have something else surface that becomes a bigger priority, and you are grateful you had not started another project already. It might be that you simply work better and feel more motivated when under pressure, as this suits your style, so delaying works well for you. Embracing procrastination positively and by-passing the fear and negative judgment it can bring can make it a workable tool in certain situations that will benefit you. You create alchemy once again, turning a potentially negative experience into a positive one.

The catch of procrastination is to make sure you are not delaying from a place of fear because you do not believe or trust in yourself. This would be another opportunity to check your beliefs if this is happening to see why doubt yourself. By kindly acknowledging that you are procrastinating and understanding that there must be a reason for this you may be more open to showing yourself why this is happening. Using self-compassion, you can then ask yourself what your reasons are for the delay. Once you understand more about the nature of your procrastination, you may be able to isolate the benefits or concerns and gently address them. Thus, you can start to become unstuck, and transform your delay into deliberation, a much more positive and considered energy that may make you feel more at ease and support you in making choices that align with your goals and wellbeing.

Perceptions power our emotions. The utility of procrastination will come down to perception, and if we perceive it negatively and put ourselves down for procrastinating, we will only add more uncomfortable emotions to manage. Adding these unnecessary feelings may then make our procrastination an even more negative experience. Procrastination can influence how we are feeling about ourselves. We may beat ourselves up emotionally for procrastinating in the first place. The more you can understand about what helps and support you, such as having more or less time pressure when completing a task or making a decision, the easier it is to set all the conditions consciously in your favour. In this way, you are less likely to create additional emotional baggage by negatively judging yourself and then possibly using yet more energy to manage this feeling. You could apply procrastination as a positive tool rather than judging it to be a negative trait. Procrastination can be a positively geared skill that enables you to have more time to reflect. This can lessen the burden of self-doubt as you are choosing to drive your procrastination, not the other way around.

When we procrastinate or get stuck in ambivalence, we can try to focus on too many things at once: too many outcomes, too many risks, too many what-ifs, all which may lead us into an overwhelming emotional state, and we then can find it harder to transform our situation. We may struggle to feel grounded and be at ease when in the procrastination or ambivalent space, and this might not support us in identifying what is really getting in our way. Is it conflicting needs or values, fear, unhelpful beliefs, self-doubt, a need for more preparation, or a need for pressure? By learning to isolate and identify our feelings this could help us map out the underlying reasons for our ambivalence or procrastination. It may help to look at any expectations we have about ourselves or our situation and see what beliefs or values might be behind them. Once we have narrowed down the beliefs or values that are getting in our way, we can look at gradually adjusting them by thinking new thoughts, again and again, as the more repeat the thoughts the more we can support opportunities for behavioural and emotional change. Remember, beliefs are just thoughts we keep thinking. So, if we have beliefs about our inability to do something, it can help to start thinking we can do it. This helps the process of building a pathway forward out of the stuck situation we might be in.

Exercise: Musical Meditation

Focusing in on our ourselves and isolating out individual emotions, expectations, beliefs and values can be difficult, even more so when our minds are split in multiple directions in a distraction-rich society. There is a lot of noise that can drown out our ability to see what sits beneath our discomfort and once we are in a state of overwhelm it becomes even harder to see the wood for the trees. But knowing what our expectations and beliefs are can be helpful in understanding our motivations, lack of motivation or why we are not content and coping. Finding those potentially unhelpful beliefs when we are being challenged in life may aid our quest in managing our wellbeing, as beliefs can be changed and redirected to support us and help reduce our emotional load once we know what they are.

The following exercise may assist you in developing a capacity to focus in on one thing at a time. By using these kinds of non-emotionally stimulating techniques to practice, our brain may develop the skill in a non-activating environment, and could then transfer this skill to other scenarios, such as isolating a feeling to see what is underneath it, work out what is the expectation and see if there could be unhelpful beliefs or a contradicting set of values there. This kind of skill, where you can focus in on what your mind is thinking and your body is feeling, can assist you in peeling back the layers to find any blocks or issues that you might otherwise not be seeing because of the mental and emotional clutter we can all experience from time to time.

Find a complex piece of music that uses multiple instruments. Classical music works well for this, or even a Queen track such as Bohemian Rhapsody. Pick one instrument at a time, like the piano, and listen only to the piano component. Exclude all the other sounds and just listen to the piano. Then shift your focus after a minute or two to another instrument and so on.

1. Find a reasonably long piece of music that uses multiple instruments; around 5 minutes is perfect.

2. Please sit comfortably, closing your eyes, and if you like, putting a hand somewhere on the body to feel connected and sense of kindness towards yourself.

3. Then focus in on one instrument at a time. Bring your awareness and attention to the sounds of that one instrument. Attempt to block out and ignore the other instruments you are hearing.

4. Repeat this process with 3 or 4 different instruments or singing voices. Each time, bring your awareness to rest on one part of the music, not the whole.

5. This could involve working with different types of sound—at the office, at the gym, at home, or while out shopping. Keep strengthening your mind's capacity to tune in to elements of complex sensory scenes to help build the parallel skill of identifying your own expectations, beliefs, and values.

Pause—Reflect—Landscape

1. Pause - Take a moment to sit with what you have just learned and consider it.

- Emotional alchemy is about transforming uncomfortable emotional states into supportive and constructive opportunities for growth and change and activating motivation.

- Ambivalence can come from contradictory feelings we cannot resolve, and if we ignore this, we may risk become stuck, feeling unmotivated and not evolving.

- Procrastination can come from being immobilised due to fears of making an incorrect decision and the possible seen and unforeseen consequences and may make motivation less accessible due to overwhelming fear.

- Working between the ego and our awareness may help us navigate out from ambivalence and procrastinating to considered action.

- Managing ambivalence and procrastination is more useful than negatively judging these states as we could waste finite resources, such as time and energy when we do this.

- Perceptions power emotions. So, if we perceive them as opportunities to make a thorough assessment of ourselves and the situation, we may be better placed to identify if we have beliefs about our capacity that are getting in the way of action.

- Starting with awareness via self-compassion, we can isolate our feelings to find the expectations that indicate we might be delaying due to self-doubt or fear.

- Once we find the beliefs or values that might be causing us some issues, we can start the gentle and gradual process of challenging and changing them, by identifying where they have come from and then adjusting them through thinking new thoughts about our capacity and circumstances that may promote our wellbeing, rather compromise it.

2. Reflect – Looking at what you have learned, and what you know about yourself, reflect on the following:

- Do you experience reductions in your motivation? Do you ever experience ambivalence? Are you someone who can procrastinate? Do you judge yourself negatively for indecision or feeling fearful?

- Do you find it easy or hard to isolate your different feelings?

- Are you used to looking at your emotions more closely or do you try to ignore them or zip through them as quickly as possible?

3. Landscape - Take a step back to see how this new information fits in with the bigger picture of your life. Consider your history, what is going on for you now, who and what is in your life, and the future you want for yourself.

- ✓ Are you able to see times in your life when you felt unmotivated, overwhelmed, stuck and unable to make decisions or changes? What was behind this? What might affect your capacity to make choices?
- ✓ When looking at your identity maps from chapter 3 are there any beliefs and values that might be contradictory and cause ambivalence or lead to procrastination? How might you go about adjusting these to promote and support your wellbeing now and in the future?

9.
In The Pursuit of Finding Balance

In this section you will be learning about:

- → Why balancing yourself on the physical, mental, emotional, and spiritual levels matters.
- → How being overly invested in balance may lead us to being unbalanced.
- → What single mindedness can do to cause us harm.
- → How to build a map to your psychodiversity with daily self-compassion.

You will need:

- ✓ Pen and paper to complete a written exercise.
- ✓ A quiet place and time to reflect.
- ✓ To be open to discussing your reactions, feelings, and ideas, either with yourself or others.

9. In The Pursuit of Finding Balance

"It's not what you look at that matters, it's what you see."
Henry David Thoreau

In school you are taught about the biology of being human, the mechanics of how your body works. You might, if you're lucky, get to know about the effects of unprotected sex and how drugs impact the body. But what no one really seems to teach you is how to balance your life well. We may know we have a brain in our heads, but we are rarely instructed on how to use it to our best advantage. We might not realise that the mind is a tool and not the boss of us, nor the font of all truth and knowledge on everything. Minds can, apparently, get it wrong. Our minds are there for us to use to enhance our lives and work in tandem with other aspects of our being: our physical self (the body and our physical health); our emotional self; our psychological self (how we see things, what we do to cope when stressed or hurt); and our intuitive, creative, or spiritual self. These are the levels we operate from as humans: physical, emotional, psychological/mental, and spiritual/creative.

To look after something, you must first know how it works. For example, we know that the sun can damage our eyes with the radiation it emits, so we wear sunglasses to protect them.

You can't fix or maintain a car without first understanding how it works. It is the same with caring for yourself. So, what occurs when we are not looking after ourselves on all the levels that we exist? What does being out of balance actually mean? What is this elusive work-life balance that we seem to keep missing? Does becoming fixated on being balanced present as much risk as being out of balance? When our minds tunnel in on one thought track, we risk excluding other possibilities and could become blinkered. This can occur in the self-caring department, where we focus on just caring for one element of who we are, or when we focus on one part of our identity. Our wellbeing could be better supported when each of the levels we experience life through, (the physical, emotional, mental and spiritual), are equally balanced and maintained. Shifts on any one level could create a domino effect that causes the other levels to become unbalanced.

For example, you are working longer hours perhaps to develop your professional identity and grow your career or to earn more money, but it is affecting your ability to sleep. As you are having trouble sleeping, this makes you physically tired, which means your brain slows down and does not operate as well. This lack of mental agility then stops you from dealing as well with your emotional problems, so you ignore your feelings as you have no energy to manage them. This inhibits your ability to be creative as you are bottling everything up and your spiritual self becomes unbalanced. You might then get sick and need more time off from the job you were trying to use to grow your career or earn more money from. Now, each level is unbalanced because you focused on only one aspect of your life, and you do not feel positive or

9. In The Pursuit of Finding Balance

good within yourself and have possibly hampered the very goals you were working towards.

Our human body and brain are ingeniously designed, and have an enormous number of component parts that work together for us to be in a cohesive existence. If we only worried about the heart and ignored the kidneys, we could still get sick from other illnesses. If we only learned academic information about how things work and did not learn to know how we feel, we could not grow and thrive. If you land on just that one identity, e.g. I am an athlete, mother, lawyer, the controlling identity or the protective identity etc., then the moment you cannot be that identity, your whole system could become at risk of collapse and emotional distress. Diversity, whether it is biodiversity, psychodiversity, or people diversity, is the richness of this world. You cannot explore all types of diversity at once, but you can weave in little microbalances that keep the ship relatively steady and your wellbeing more keenly balanced.

Imbalances can show themselves in all sorts of guises, from the micro or macro view. We can lose our temper over a slow driver in front of us, triggering road rage, because we did not take in the bigger picture (macro view) that this is an 80-year-old who prefers care and caution over driving faster, also neglecting to realise that we, too, will be 80 one day, and probably will still want to drive and be independent without being yelled at by impatient younger drivers in a rush. We can miss a much broader perspective still, that we have in fact, encountered 30 other drivers today who did not annoy us, so, really, the numbers are on our side. Sometimes we lose our tempers because we simply needed an outlet to do so. The road rage is just a channel for what was already out of balance. But, there might be a more effective way to manage that balance without taking it out on 80-year-old drivers.

When you have a strong emotional response, it is telling you something. Learn to listen to your body and mind to find out what that is. Gently and kindly correct the imbalance when you can, and be in a place of compassion, acceptance and patience when you can't. It could be something as simple as your hormone levels are going through a phase. This happens to us all, and whilst you may not be able to influence your hormone levels easily, mindful management of what hormonal fluctuations do to your behaviour and emotions could help you to navigate situations from a place of self-compassion. You can't necessarily directly influence or change your hormone levels, though what you eat, exercising and other behaviours may sometimes help. But even just knowing this is what it is going on for you, means that you can take extra care to be kind to yourself and others. That's a good starting place.

The **more psychodiverse** you are in your **approach to your self-care**, the more you increase capacity and opportunity for managing and maintaining your sense of balance. Another metaphor for psychodiversity would be to consider the photographer, who has an array of different lenses that have varying focal lengths for a reason. It allows them to capture all kinds of shots: close ups, panoramas, fisheye, and high-speed motion. Your perception and self-care tools could benefit from the same array of lenses with which you view, access, and manage yourself and your life. This is the psychodiversity of the mind: the ability to switch out your lenses as the situation changes and create better internal balance. For example, you might have started by doing some close-up work on being more creative, but in the process, you have then stepped away from being active and, after a while, your body starts to feel sore, stiff, and de-energised. Taking a wide-angle and broader view, you can see that creativity has come at the cost of physical activity. Therefore, you can step back and add in a good, long walk every day for a counterbalance. In the process of walking, you encounter different visuals that later then inspire your creativity.

Maintaining your balance, whilst important, is also something you must be careful not to become obsessed with. There will be times when you naturally slip out of balance. It is very normal for humans to come in and out of their equilibrium or have less time and resources available for one area of their lives. Judging or criticising yourself for it will not help matters and could deplete precious resources of energy. It is all part of the dance of life, and being aware and present may well help you keep an eye on that balance and step in to make relevant change before do yourself harm. We are, by nature, always changing and aging. Therefore, our requirements to maintain balance will naturally change. It can help us to be ready and alert to adapt to an ever-changing existence by being aware and having access to an array of coping tools. Sometimes, we can learn a lot when things go wrong or are hard for us. Seeing challenges as a negative might not empower us to make the most of every opportunity that comes our way. Thinking how **everything shows us something** could open up possibilities for growth and change.

By being aware that when you feel a strong, uncomfortable emotion, or you are not at your best physically, or your creativity is blocked, or you are unable to focus your mind, could all be possible indications that some area of your life is out of balance and may increase your chances to do something about that lack of balance. Balance is unique to everyone, and what works for someone else may not work for you. You must harmonise with what can work for you. Your knowledge about you, about what works and what does not, is your psychodiversity map, and it may lead to adapting according to your needs to sustain a more-balanced life.

Exercise: Balance Check-Up

The exercise below could be a helpful check-up for seeing what you are doing in the important areas of your life and identifying if anything needs re-balancing. This may help support you in being mindful of meeting and managing these needs, and it could be worth re-visiting regularly. Just as you might see the doctor for a physical check-up, do a balance check-up. If you are feeling out of balance, maybe come back to this check-up and see if you have started to neglect any areas of late or if you need to increase activity in one domain.

1. Psychological wellbeing - *Managing self-criticism, rumination, negative overthinking, and hyper-focusing.* How are you supporting your mind at present? What helps when you are stressed (e.g., closing your eyes and resting, breathing exercises, meditation, having fun, talking to someone)? Can you think of other ways to get out of you head that are safe and sustainable?

2. Physical wellbeing - *Nurturing, feeding, moving, and relaxing the body.* How are you currently looking after yourself physically (e.g., good food, exercise, dancing, walking, massage, warm bath, resting)? Are there new ways you want to explore caring for your physical wellbeing? Can others help you with them?

3. Emotional wellbeing - *Supporting, encouraging, and nurturing yourself.* How do you care for yourself emotionally (e.g., talking kindly to yourself, finding someone or an animal to hug, giving to others, seeking help)? Do you need to adopt some new ways to be compassionate and caring towards yourself? Do you make space and time to be with your feelings and gently explore and understand them?

4. Creative wellbeing - *Exploring your imagination and emotional expression through creative acts.* How do you support your creative or spiritual side (e.g., laughing, being in nature, cooking, painting, meditation)? Have you seen creative pursuits you would like to try, or is your fear of not being good enough blocking you from trying new things? Can you be creative for the sake of creativity without it needing to be a masterpiece?

5. Relationship wellbeing - Have you made time for your relationships lately (e.g., spending time together, playing games, getting in touch with individuals directly instead of being on your devices)? Can you safely be more vulnerable in some of your relationships to build greater intimacy and support for one another?

Pause—Reflect—Landscape

1. Pause - Take a moment to sit with what you have just learned and consider it.

- It can be helpful to recognise we both experience and operate from the physical, emotional, psychological and spiritual/creative aspects of ourselves.

- Mindful management of all these 4 aspects equally may assist us in creating balance and maintaining inner harmony.

- Being out of balance and not caring well for one domain could affect the others and cascade us into a state of dis-ease and cause problems.

- Caring for and managing all our identities or roles we have in life can help us to maintain a healthier balance.

- Strong emotional reactions could be an indicator that our internal balance is off. Checking our perspective on our physical, emotional, psychological and spiritual/creative health might provide answers and directions for remedying imbalances to support our overall wellbeing.

- We must check that our quest for balance does not overtake our capacity to be in the moment and flow with the joy of life. Hyper-focusing on balance may create an imbalance and is as potentially unhelpful as not checking in ourselves.

2. Reflect – Looking at what you have learned, and what you know about yourself, reflect on the following:

- Are you someone who is mindful of your physical, emotional, psychological or creative health?
- Do you have any tendencies to hyper-focus on one or all domains and veer into unhealthy perfectionism or high expectations?
- Do you find it hard to care for yourself in one in these domains?

3. Landscape - Take a step back to see how this new information fits in with the bigger picture of your life. Consider your history, what is going on for you now, who and what is in your life, and the future you want for yourself.

- ✓ Can you see times where you have neglected one domain of life, be it the physical, mental, emotional or spiritual, and suffered with consequences from this? Is there something you can learn from this?
- ✓ What can influence how much attention you pay to each of these domains? Is this a helpful or unhelpful influence?
- ✓ If there are some domains that are easier for you to look after than others, can you see why this is and use some of this information to support more care in other areas?

9. In The Pursuit of Finding Balance

- ✓ What could you do to remove any blocks, or break down any barriers to making sure you pay attention equally to your physical, emotional, psychological and spiritual/creative wellbeing?

10. Review of Insights into You

We have introduced the idea of creating our own adaptable sustainable psychology approach to life, one that can flex and grow as both we and our environment change. Encouraging the sourcing of sustainable ways of coping to help deal with the inevitable challenges that come with being human.

We have looked at the many ways in which our mental and emotional wellbeing may be influenced, both positively and negatively, and that the more we know about ourselves, the easier it could become to see which of those influences may help us and which could harm us. We have discussed how identity can be multi-faceted and complex and could include an identity that we develop and direct into taking care of ourselves. We have explored how it might aid us to **balance self-focus with self-forgetting**, moving between recognising and caring for others' needs and our own.

We have started the process of mapping out how we see ourselves, what we believe to be true about ourselves, what supports us and what doesn't, identifying what our strengths are, and looking to see how they can **support us in finding courage and capacity** to compassionately challenge limiting beliefs and gradually change unhelpful behaviours. By acknowledging our strengths, we might see ways in which they could support our vulnerabilities and help us to care for ourselves with gentleness and kindness.

Consciousness is how much we are able to be present in any given moment and can be accessed through both the ego state and our awareness. The ego can be very singularly focused and may limit us in terms of how we assess ourselves and our achievements. The ego can also help motivate us into accessing new opportunities that could lead us into further growth and creativity. Awareness is the state where we might enter and discover a greater level of inner peace and self-acceptance. Allowing us potentially to find self-trust and provide support in making decisions that could facilitate change and adaptation. **Giving and receiving compassion** may assist in mediating our ability to move between the ego and awareness and this may assist us on our path to care for our mental and emotional wellbeing.

We have broached the subject of assuming our negative beliefs about ourselves to be always true as potentially being unhelpful and unsustainable. We may need to exercise more caution and consider assessing whether believing our negative or positive attributes is supportive, or if it could lead to limiting our capacity to move into a state of change. **Questioning the validity of our assumptions**, checking that we aren't hiding anything from ourselves or allowing self-doubt to dictate how we feel about ourselves may assist in managing the impact of any negative influences.

We have reviewed and built some understanding about how our emotions may come from our behaviours, that our behaviour can be driven by what we think about, and that our thoughts can be created through our core beliefs and values. These beliefs and values can stem from our core nature, our experiences (from parents, education, events, etc.), from the culture and society we are immersed in, and from how others have treated us. Whilst we might have held these beliefs as being absolutely true, sometimes they might not be. Fortunately, our **beliefs can be changed** gradually with care and compassionate support.

We have explored how our perception of ourselves and events is continually under our control. This means that when something very challenging or painful occurs we may be able to offer ourselves some support and assistance by compassionately altering our perceptions and this may create changes in our feelings. This might not be easy or simple, but being kind to and supportive of ourselves can be enough to make a difference. By understanding who we are, why we do what we do, and where this could lead us into trouble, we can begin to develop appropriate strategies to manage this. **The impact of influences can be adjusted when they are recognised and understood.**

There may be times in our lives that we can hide things, even from ourselves, and create identities based on how we wish to appear to be to ourselves or others. This can be done through pretence or self-deception. There is no value in judging this behaviour negatively and by compassionately unmasking, privately to ourselves, we can create an opportunity to forge a closer connection to our authentic inner self. This may well help us build self-trust and could assist us in healing past pain, increasing our self-worth, affording us the opportunity to learn how to **value the person we are,** not who we pretend to be. Being considerate of how we are received by ourselves and other people rather than perceived, could assist in supporting how we manage self-doubt and identify risks of self-deception.

If we become self-phobic, then we may find it harder to build an authentic relationship with ourselves and this may even lead us towards a path of self-sabotage if our self-phobia is founded in a feeling of not being worthy or good enough. Self-phobia can cause an unease or dislike of being around ourselves and may show up through constant distraction or busyness, or a curated real or virtual persona to hide behind. It could be we fear knowing more about ourselves or fear the surfacing of unpleasant or even traumatic memories. To help us in untangling the webs of fearing ourselves, or any self-deception, pretence and self-sabotage, we might consider traveling through the world of our expectations. By looking at our expectations of ourselves and others, this might reveal useful information about our beliefs and values, and how, at times, we may be unconsciously working against ourselves.

Being a metacognition, thinking about our thinking can lead us towards understanding the hidden and complex aspects of ourselves that might not be supporting us in taking care of our mental and emotional wellbeing. By looking more closely at our ways of thinking, we could access important knowledge about ourselves. This knowledge may become useful in supporting us to create a more sustainable sense of calm and feeling into a place of self-acceptance. **By giving us a map to ourselves that could help us to navigate through life** from a perspective of clearly knowing what supports our mental and emotional wellbeing, and what does not.

We have ventured into the concept of emotional alchemy, considering the potential benefits of transforming uncomfortable emotions into opportunities for learning and supporting our future emotional sustainability. We have begun the work of developing a clearer picture of when our emotions may be driven from our ego's behaviours, and which may stem from our awareness. Recognising that, sometimes, our ego's beliefs and needs might result in us becoming ambivalent and stuck in ideas and ideals, rather than focusing on what supports us and what does not.

We have talked about how we may use tools like procrastination to positively serve us through using the non-judgmental

10. Review of Insights into You

prism of awareness and turn what could be perceived as negative state into a **growth asset**. As negative judgment or criticism of ourselves can be a cause of mental and emotional fatigue, by cutting out the noise of our self-doubt we may be able to access a clearer view of ourselves, and this might reveal ways to support us that we had not previously seen.

We have highlighted the value in recognising that we experience life through a physical, emotional, psychological and spiritual lens and that caring for all these aspects could assist us in our quest for balance and maintaining inner harmony. Either being out of balance or not caring for one of these domains could negatively impact the others and cause other issues for us. By caring well for all the identities, roles and lenses through which we experience life we may develop a balanced sense of well-being. Being mindful that, at the same time, we do not hyperfocus on the concept of balance, as this could in itself create an imbalance or other problems for us to manage.

We have sat with and explored the concept of what self-compassion is and what it might look like for us as individuals. Understanding that by using this lens of self-compassion, we may find it easier to identify when we are constructing a negative view of ourselves, and we are being unfairly harsh or having unreasonable expectations on ourselves. Some of which may have originated from the influences of experiences, media or other people. Hopefully we have explained that **by showing yourself kindness,** it opens up the possibility for growth and healing to begin and continue.

Exercise: Insights Gained into You

Now, go back over the exercises you have completed, the reflections you have experienced and the insights you have gained, and answer the following questions. The information gathered here will help form the basis for the next part of this work, and may improve your retention of any learning or insights gained.

1. What have you learned about yourself and how your perception of yourself has been influenced by experiences, people or the media?
2. What are your strengths, and can you use them to help you change things you do not like about yourself, or support areas where you could be vulnerable to being hurt by others or put yourself down?
3. Do you have beliefs about yourself that are harming you? Or do you have values that contradict your beliefs and cause you problems? Where have those beliefs and values come from? Are they absolutely true, or relatively true? Do you find it easy or hard to have self-compassion for the things you dislike about yourself?

4. Which beliefs, values, and expectations belong to ego? How can your awareness help manage these so they can be used positively to support growth and change?

5. Have you noticed any trends of judging yourself unhelpfully when you are not like others, or not achieving certain standards? Is this something you are prepared to challenge and change? Do you think such habits come from the ego or awareness?

6. What have you learned about your expectations? Are they reasonable and fair on you and others? Can you now work out how to find the belief and values that sit behind an expectation?

7. Have you identified if there are areas of your life where you might be practicing self-deception or using too much pretence? Does this behaviour cause you to miss unhelpful habits that need working on or wounds that need healing? Can you move into self-sabotaging behaviours?

8. Do you experience ambivalence in any areas of life and if yes, what are the beliefs and values you have that may block changing this? Do you procrastinate, and if so, do you judge this negatively or use the space and time to help make more considered choices?

9. How confident do you feel in recognising your emotions? Or picking up unhelpful lines of thought that are negative in nature? Is this a skill you may need to work on and improve to help support your mental and emotional wellbeing?

10. What does a balanced life look like for you in each of the 4 domains, physical, emotional, psychological and spiritual/creative? What signs tell you balance is not there, and how can you support yourself in managing this?

Next Steps

With this reflective work of developing your own adaptable sustainable psychology, this collection of books invites you to consider who you have been in past, who you are in the present, and how you would like to be in the future. Exploring ideas and strategies that may be of assistance to you in promoting and maintaining your wellbeing. Offering support in discovering the balance between self-acceptance and the motivation to evolve, without falling into the trap of self-improvement burnout. Learning, that by attuning to your own needs you may feel more able to meet the needs of others, and this could help you set clearer boundaries that reflect emotional safety and create supportive relationships.

This first book of the interactive series has set out to assist you in opening a space to explore how experiences, people, and media may affect how you feel about yourself. We have discussed how cultivating an increased self-awareness, you can begin to focus on supporting yourself in ways that align with your personal strengths and values, so you're better equipped to care for your vulnerabilities and adapt through life's challenges.

Having come through this first part, you may be beginning to recognise:

10. Review of Insights into You

- What you're feeling may not be the whole picture.
- Who you are is not necessarily the problem.
- The challenge may lie in how you've been shaped or made to feel by external influences.
- Knowing yourself well can support choices that promote your wellbeing.

By understanding how repeated exposure to certain ideas, messages, or expectations can shape beliefs and values, whether or not they serve your long-term wellbeing, you may begin to gently deconstruct identity patterns that have been influenced by others or experiences. This journey is not about quick fixes or following someone else's blueprint for change. It's about making space for you to be able to reflect, reframe, and gradually shift toward ways of being that feel sustainable and supportive for you.

Book 2: **I'm Getting There – *Overcoming emotional obstacles and hidden patterns that can block change*** builds on these foundations by exploring how unhelpful thinking patterns, such as negative self-talk or holding unfair expectations upon ourselves, might be recognised and compassionately addressed. Drawing on insights from neuroscience and your own self-reflection, we examine how repeated, intentional actions may support changing habits and could develop emotional resilience. Returning to the emotional landscape, this section explores ideas to help you care for yourself in adaptive, sustainable ways that respect your individuality and lived experience.

Acknowledgments - With Gratitude

I would like to respectfully acknowledge and thank all the individuals who have inspired, created, and contributed to our current body of psychological knowledge. This book draws on the brilliant work of many who have postulated theories, tested them, or created therapeutic techniques to help those in distress.

My deepest thanks go to every client I've had the privilege of working with. Each interaction has been a valuable learning experience, teaching me more about how humans are shaped by one another and the world around them.

I would like to thank my parents, who have provided a backdrop of consistent support. I am deeply fortunate and blessed to have been inspired by my mother's constant capacity for forgiveness and care, and by my father's determination to keep moving forward, no matter the obstacles.

I'm incredibly grateful to my dedicated, kind, hard-working, and funny partner, Andy. Knowing his love and support is there as a constant, and receiving his encouragement when things have been difficult, has made an enormous difference over the past few years.

To all my friends, thank you—particularly Talina, who has never doubted me and has been a steady stream of support, encouragement, and kindness. I'm also super grateful for my long-term school friends Kerry, Katie, and Laura, whose wisdom, humour, and compassion carry me through life's challenges. And to Jim, whose company has been one of the greatest blessings—offering nourishment, fun, learning, and the simple joy of sharing life.

I would like to express my gratitude and respect to my mentor and supervisor, Dr. Bruce Wilson, for his care and guidance over the years; to Helen and Alex for their generosity, intelligence, and skills in promoting this work; and to Kerry for her editing talents, positive support, and insightful guidance.

I'm extremely thankful to everyone at Author Services Australia who helped bring this book to life. Regardless of the outcome, I'm truly pleased with what we've created - thanks in large part to the brilliant, patient, and hard-working individuals who put up with my endless list of revisions.

My final acknowledgment goes to my first husband. While I lost you on the 12th day of the 12th month in 2012 – a day where so much of my world ended - I have from that awful moment been continually supported by the love we shared, the hope you gave me, and your constant belief in what I could achieve. I would not be who I am without you.